THE STORY OF MOSES MENDELSSOHN
(1729-1786)

The Story of

MOSES
MENDELSSOHN

A Biography for Young People

by
JACQUELINE PINTO

LONDON
VALLENTINE · MITCHELL

Published by
VALLENTINE, MITCHELL & CO., LTD.
37, Furnival Street, London, E.C.4.

© Jacqueline Pinto 1960

Made and printed in Great Britain
by C. Tinling & Co. Ltd.
Liverpool, London and Prescot

Contents

TO JOE

CHAPTER ONE

The Great Decision

THERE was silence in the main hall of the public seminary of Dessau. Twenty boys were sitting on the wooden benches, waiting for their teacher to work himself up into one of his not infrequent rages. As he strode forward to the front of the room and faced them all, the storm broke.

'*Who* threw that book? Which one of you dares to insult your school . . . your religion . . . your God? Who is it among you who cares so little for our sacred heritage that he allows our most holy book to lie defiled in the dust on this floor?'

Herr Abram's face was now purple. As he shook with anger, his long white beard swayed. Moses Mendelssohn, a small, hunchbacked pupil, thought he would laugh if he watched that beard much longer. He stood up.

'I'm awfully sorry, sir. I'm afraid it was me. It was an accident, though. I just picked up the book – I didn't think of it being a Bible – and before I knew

9

A*

what was happening, it was flying across the room
– straight for Joseph's head. I *suppose* I must have
thrown it, but it all happened so quickly that I can't
quite remember exactly what I did.'

There was a titter from the back of the class.
Joseph had threatened to drop a spider down Moses'
neck, and as he had slowly advanced, Moses had
flung the book . . . and in had walked Herr Abram.

'SILENCE! I do not accept your explanation. I
think you deliberately picked up the Holy Bible,
caring so little for its teachings—'

'That's not true,' interrupted Moses indignantly.
'You know that's not true!'

'I know nothing of the sort. I only know that you
are a rude and difficult pupil, whom it is my mis-
fortune to instruct. But to-day I shall not waste my
time and my efforts in teaching one who flings the
sacred words of God in the dust. . . .'

Moses sighed with exasperation. It was impossible
to reason with Herr Abram. You just had to wait for
the storm to subside—and goodness knows how long
this one was going to take.

However, it ended sooner than anyone expected.
Herr Abram was in a hurry to get home that evening
to comfort his wife. For weeks there had been rumours that her brother had left Poland, and they
believed he might make his way to the state of
Anhalt, of which Dessau was the capital. Every day
they waited anxiously for news, but none came.
Young Jews who were conscripted into Poland's

army suffered dreadful hardships: many tried to flee from their country—but not all succeeded.

Herr Abram's head ached. He and his wife had talked of nothing but her brother for weeks; now he was tired and strained, and in no mood to cope with his high-spirited pupils.

'Moses, I will not allow you to remain in my class to-day. You are to go home and tell your parents of your bad conduct. In the meantime, I will report this to Rabbi Frankel. I have no doubt he will have more to say to you about this to-morrow.'

'But, sir, I . . .'

'We will not discuss this any longer. Leave the room immediately.'

There was nothing Moses could do but obey. Frowning, he took his cloak from the peg. As he walked past the benches, Joseph hissed sympathetically, 'Sorry about this. Bet you'll be for it to-morrow with Frankel. Still, you've got the afternoon off, lucky devil.'

'SILENCE!' thundered Herr Abram for the second time that day, and there was not another word until Moses left the room.

It was a crisp October day, and as Moses walked sadly down the narrow street towards his home, he pulled his almost threadbare cloak more tightly round himself. His black trousers had been made out of an old pair of his father's knee-breeches, and his shoes had been so well worn that his toes were coming through the top. Although Moses was twelve

11

years old – he was born on 6th September, 1729 – he looked so small and frail that people took him to be much younger. His jet-black hair and dark eyes seemed to accentuate his pallid complexion; but his high, intelligent forehead, and eager, enquiring expression distinguished him from his fellows.

As he walked on past the shabby, broken-down buildings, his thoughts turned from his own troubles to those of his people. It seemed so unfair that Jews had to live in poverty, confined within a ghetto. Why should they lead such narrow lives when other people could walk, work, and make their homes wherever they wished?

Yet in Dessau Jews were treated better than in many other parts of Germany – or Prussia, as it was then called. At least, here, they were allowed to have their own synagogue, public baths, hospital, school, and cemetery. But in some places Jews were not allowed to live at all; and in others, even in the city of Frankfort, Moses had been told, angry mobs would storm the ghettoes, murder men, women and children, ransack the buildings and leave the narrow streets in ruins.

In the year 1741 – when this story opens – the German attitude to the Jews was (as it had been for many hundreds of years) cruel and intolerant. In the principalities where Jews were tolerated, they were taxed with incredible harshness, they suffered from all kinds of restrictions, they were not allowed to travel freely from one place to another, they could not attend universities, nor could they enter the professions. They were expected merely to eke out a humble existence by becoming pedlars, dealers in old clothes, money-lenders—or just beggars!

It was all completely, utterly wrong, decided Moses, as he turned the corner and continued down the cobbled street. His legs were aching now – he was not strong, and sometimes the short walk between school and home seemed unending.

Moses wondered what his parents would say when they knew the reason for his early return. His father would probably still be busy, either with the few young pupils to whom he taught the Torah, or with copying Hebrew scrolls in his exquisite handwriting for which he was well known among the Jewish community of Dessau.

At last Moses reached his house – a small, stone building at the end of a narrow courtyard. He pulled open the wooden front door, and stepped inside the dark, cheerless hall. 'Hello, Mother!' he called.

'Moses! Why are you home at this time? Are you all right?' Inside the kitchen, a medium-sized room in which the family cooked, ate, sat, and washed, Frau Mendel put down her baking-tin and rushed into the hall. She was a slightly-built, tired-looking woman, dressed in a shabby, ankle-length black gown, which was tied round her waist. She kissed her son and looked at him anxiously.

'Of course I am. I suppose Father's busy?' Moses took off his cloak and hung it up carefully in the hall.

'I don't think he'll be long, dear. Come into the kitchen. I've been making some bread this after-noon.'

Moses followed his mother inside. 'Ummm! No wonder there's such a lovely smell in here. Can I have a bit?'

'Yes, but only a little. I want it to last for a few days. We mustn't talk too loudly, as it will disturb your father. He's been busy in his workroom all day long.'

Opposite the kitchen, on the other side of the hall (which itself was just wide enough for one person to stand in) was a small, low-ceilinged room in which Herr Mendel spent most of his time. It was sparsely furnished, with a few chairs, a battered table and some shelves for books and parchments.

Herr Mendel had been working since six o'clock that morning, first with his pupils, then with trans-cribing on parchment the Hebrew words of the Pentateuch, and now he felt his labours deserved a break. Also he had heard Moses speaking to his mother in the kitchen, and he wondered why the boy had come home so early from school.

He stood up, put his books and scrolls away, then went into the kitchen. Herr Mendel was a small man with greying hair and beard, and with a lined face. He looked as though he could do with a good square meal – but that was a thing the Mendel family could rarely afford. His brows knit anxiously as he saw his son.

14

'You're home early, Moses. Weren't you feeling well?' Moses' health had always been a worry to him –when the child was very small, he used to wrap him up in an old cloak and carry him to school. Moses had become stronger as the years had passed, and the stammer which impeded his speech had lessened slightly, but he would never be as fit as other boys.

'I'm all right, but there was some trouble this afternoon, and Abey sent me home – mainly, I think, because he was in a bad mood.' Moses then told them about the spider, the Bible, and the sudden appearance of Herr Abram.

Moses recounted the story so amusingly that his parents could not help laughing. 'Well, I don't think it was such a serious crime, though that is certainly not the way to treat a holy book,' said his father, thinking of all the back-breaking hours he had spent copying sacred writings. 'But this does rather bring things to a head, Moses,' he went on, now without a smile on his face. 'Your mother and I have talked it over very carefully, and we think you should soon leave school and start earning some money. We know how interested you are in your lessons and that you think you would like to become a rabbi, but it's no good, Moses. That sort of life would not do for you. There are too many Talmudic students and rabbis in Prussia, and most of them have a desperately hard time making ends meet. Now, if you will listen to your mother and me, you can lead a far more comfortable life. Give up this idea of studying Hebrew, and become a pedlar.'

'Father, you *know* I couldn't! I should hate to go round selling things. Anyway, I wouldn't be any good at it because I could never persuade people to buy something they didn't want. I don't mind about earning a lot of money: I would much rather do what I want instead.'

Frau Mendel put her hand to her forehead and sighed. 'Moses, dear, you must listen to us. We know what it is like to live in poverty, to marry, to have children – and never to have enough to eat or drink, or sufficient clothes to wear.'

'I know, Mother, I know! But you and Father managed somehow, and I don't see why I shouldn't do the same.'

'You are too young to understand, Moses,' said his father sternly. 'You will have to do what you are told. You may stay at the seminary until you are a little older, then you must leave. Your mother and I love you very much – and it is because of our love that we wish you to have a better life than we have had. There's no reason why you should not continue to study in the evenings, or whenever you have the time. You don't have to forget your books once you leave school, but you must remember that you have responsibilities towards your parents just as they have towards you. You must soon start contributing to our family income.'

Moses listened quietly, his eyes fixed steadfastly

on his father's face. Then he said in a low voice, 'I want to study. I *won't* be a pedlar. You *can't* make me.' His voice trembled, but remained determined. '*Please* understand!'

His parents eyed each other helplessly. They were at a loss for words. Moses had made up his mind . . . how could they change it?

Frowning, his father turned away and, with a slight shake of his head, left the room.

Moses appealed to his mother. 'Can't you see,' he cried passionately, 'that you and Father are wrong? It's *my* life, and I must lead it the way *I* think best.'

But his mother made no response. Torn between the wishes of her husband and herself and the fervent desires of her son, she could think of no words of reason or comfort.

Slowly Moses walked towards the door, then went into the hall and climbed the steep, dark stairs to the little room which he shared with his brothers, Saul and Jente. He went over to the window and sat, shaking and exhausted, with his head buried in his arms upon the sill. It was no good. What was he to do? He would never be able to make his parents change their minds – and God knew he could never change his.

He sat motionless for a long time. Then he raised his head and stared unhappily out of the window. He watched someone in a broad-brimmed black hat and long black cloak hurrying down the courtyard. Suddenly Moses leant forward and gasped with astonishment. He *thought* it was Rabbi David Frankel coming towards their house. Moses looked closer. It *was*!

He jumped up and rushed to the door of his room, but by the time he had reached the stairs his father, who had also seen the visitor approach, was welcoming him into the house.

Herr Mendel shook hands with his distinguished guest. 'Rabbi Frankel, this is indeed an honour. My wife will be delighted when I tell her you are here, although we very much regret the reason for your coming. I'm afraid Moses caused some trouble at school to-day, but I am sure he is very sorry. . . .'

Rabbi Frankel raised his hand in protest, and smiled gently. 'My dear Mendel, do not apologise for your son. It was an unfortunate but not uncommon incident of school life. I have not come to discuss that with you, but to speak to you instead about Moses' future.'

Herr Mendel looked puzzled. 'Well, would you please come into my workroom and I will call my wife.' He held open the door for the rabbi, and then went into the kitchen.

Moses was flabbergasted. He watched his mother and father disappear into the workroom, then he sighed with relief as he saw the door had been left slightly ajar. He couldn't resist standing where he was and waiting for the sound of voices to float up to him.

'Your son is very gifted,' Moses heard Rabbi

Frankel say. 'I would like to promote him to my special class and give him more tuition in the Torah. You see, I think Moses has a great future: during all my years of teaching, I have never come across a boy who is so anxious to learn, who is so quick to understand, and who is so capable of original thought.'

Moses then heard his father speak. 'But, Rabbi Frankel, my wife and I are most concerned about all this. We think Moses should soon leave school and become a pedlar. He is not strong, yet day after day and night after night we find him straining over his books.'

'Yes, that's quite true,' agreed Frau Mendel. 'Do you know, Rabbi, he spends hours poring over Moses Maimonides' book, *Guide to the Perplexed*. It can't be right for a child to spend so long reading and thinking about things which must be beyond his understanding.'

'Frau Mendel, it is because it *is* so right that I have come to see you. Moses is an exceptional scholar, and I feel I cannot leave this house until I have persuaded you to allow your son to continue his studies.'

Moses waited no longer. With shining eyes and with his whole face transformed with happiness, he almost danced back into his room. A few moments ago, he had been in the depths of despair: now his joy and excitement knew no bounds. He had such confidence in Rabbi Frankel – he knew his parents would give way.

19

He went over to a little table – the only furniture in the room, apart from a couple of chairs, and a medium-sized bed in which the three brothers slept – and picked up a book. He sat down on the bed and smiled as he turned over the pages – poor Mother, she could never understand why he always liked Maimonides' *Guide to the Perplexed*. No one could be more perplexed than she! Stopping at random, he laboriously read:

> Free will is granted to every man. If he wishes to direct himself toward the good way and become righteous, the will to do so is in his hand; and if he wishes to direct himself toward the bad way and become wicked, the will to do so is likewise in his hand. Thus it is written in the Torah: 'Behold, the man is become as one of us, knowing good and evil' – that is to say, the human species has become unique in the world in that it can know of itself, by its own wit and reflection, what is good and what is evil, and in that it can do whatever it wishes.

Moses lay back on the hard bed. He felt as though Maimonides had written that paragraph especially for him. 'I do want to "direct myself toward the good way and become righteous,"' he whispered to himself.

It was a strange and wonderful thing, thought Moses, to read the words of a man who had lived in the twelfth century, yet who seemed so up-to-date. 'I'd like to be a philosopher, too,' Moses decided. 'I'd like to be able to write about important things so that, centuries hence, boys of twelve will read the things I have said – just as I am reading Maimonides to-day.'

Half an hour later, Moses heard from below the sound of chairs being scraped back, then muffled voices as Rabbi Frankel said good-bye. He lay still on the bed, then sat up as he heard his father's footsteps on the stairs. His bedroom door opened.

'Moses, did you know Rabbi Frankel was coming to speak to us about you?'

'No, Father, I didn't, but I saw him from the window as he walked towards the house.'

Luckily his father did not ask whether Moses had heard any of the conversation that had followed: he was far too intent upon what he had to say. 'Rabbi Frankel has persuaded your mother and me to allow you to continue at school. He is so sure that your only chance of happiness lies in the study of great and holy works that I have decided to let you make your own choice. But, Moses, before you finally decide, I beg you to consider all that such a decision might mean. You are not strong, and since birth you have suffered from what the physicians call a curvature of the spine. This will not get better – indeed it may get worse if you spend your days bending over your books instead of walking in the open air and working as a pedlar.

'Think over what I have said, Moses. Be very sure that you are prepared to face poverty – and, possibly, starvation—in order merely to improve your mind.'

Herr Mendel looked weary. He felt positive that

Rabbi Frankel was wrong – wrong to think that Moses had such exceptional gifts, and wrong to encourage the boy to endure great hardships in the future.

'I do not need to think it over, Father,' replied Moses, and never in his life had his voice held such conviction. 'I want – more than anything else in the world – to go on studying.'

CHAPTER TWO

Onward to Berlin

FOR the past two years Moses had enjoyed every minute of his life at the seminary. Since his promotion to Rabbi Frankel's class he had progressed very quickly, and nothing seemed dull or too difficult for his eager brain. Formerly he had spent his time studying Hebrew grammar, and learning mechanically long Biblical passages, and long lists of instructions about such things as marriage, divorce and legal damages. But now his lessons had taken on a new meaning: he could understand the Torah and the Talmud, he could write poetry in Hebrew, and he had mastered the Scriptures. Rabbi Frankel made work even more interesting by going through Moses Maimonides' *Guide to the Perplexed,* explaining the thoughts and conclusions of this great philosopher in a way which the young Moses could understand.

Moses had never regretted his decision to keep on studying, although he was still not sure what he wanted to do when he left school. To his parents' secret dismay, his enthusiasm for his lessons increased. He still stayed up late each night exhausting himself both physically and mentally with his study of rabbinic literature, but he enjoyed it all so much that he scarcely noticed his tiredness the following morning or the pain in his humped back.

One day, in the spring of 1743, Moses reached school and found the boys in his class standing together talking quietly, instead of playing about as they usually did. He did not take much notice of this until he shouted 'Hello' to Joseph, and Joseph opened his mouth to reply but no sound came out.

Moses laughed. 'I always said you'd lose your voice one day through talking too much. Now we'll all be able to get a word in for a change.'

'You'd better tell him, Joseph,' muttered David, a solemn, pale-faced boy who was standing next to him. 'He'll have to know sooner or later, and it might as well be now.'

'Tell me what?' asked Moses.

'Well . . .' Joseph said hesitatingly and stopped. Then he decided to tell Moses the whole story and finish with it. 'You know Sam's father is quite friendly with Rabbi Frankel, don't you? Well,' he went on, all in one breath and without waiting for Moses to reply, 'he saw Frankel last night, and he told Sam this morning that Frankel has been appointed Chief Rabbi of Berlin.'

Moses stared at Joseph, his eyes opened wide with astonishment, and said nothing.

'That means,' went on Joseph awkwardly, 'that Rabbi Frankel will be going to live in Berlin. I think he's leaving Dessau quite soon.'

Still Moses said nothing. He was, in fact, too numb with shock to speak. Suddenly his safe, happy world had fallen to pieces. He turned away so that Joseph should not see the tears in his eyes.

Later on in the morning Rabbi Frankel confirmed Joseph's story. He had been called to Berlin, and while he was naturally pleased at the great honour, his pride at his new appointment was mixed with sorrow at the thought of leaving Dessau. As he spoke, Rabbi Frankel glanced across the room, and his eyes rested for a second on Moses' bent head. Then he realised why Moses had been so quiet and strained that morning – obviously he had already heard the news, and was afraid it would affect his education.

Moses did not join in the questions that were showered upon the Rabbi about his new work. With an effort, he gave the faintest glimmer of a smile when Joseph tried to cheer him up. 'It won't be so bad once he's actually gone, Moses,' he whispered. 'It'll give you and Abey a chance to renew your friendship! Anyway, we'll all be leaving school soon.'

But Joseph's words of comfort did not help. The day dragged wearily by. For the first time since he had been promoted to Rabbi Frankel's class, Moses felt no interest or pleasure in his work. For the first time he longed for the day to end so that he could escape from school into the bright sunshine outside. 'It ought to be raining,' thought Moses. 'If I controlled the heavens there would be a positive downpour!'

Moses was usually among the few boys who stayed behind after school, asking Rabbi Frankel more questions on the day's lessons and probing more deeply into the teachings of the Talmud. To-day he was the first to put his books away and leave the seminary.

A week later Rabbi Frankel left Dessau. On the morning that he was due to depart Moses left home even earlier than usual and walked some distance down the road along which Rabbi Frankel's coach would pass. Desperately unhappy, he stood waiting and watching, and when at last the coach came trundling along Moses' self-control gave way and he burst into a flood of tears. Sobbing bitterly, he watched the coach as it went past him.

Suddenly there was a shout from inside the coach, the horse reared up as the reins were pulled, and someone leaned out of the carriage. 'Why, Moses!' said a familiar voice. 'I thought it must be you!'

Then, with a murmured word to the coachman, Rabbi Frankel jumped down and came swiftly over to Moses. 'You mustn't cry like this,' he said quietly. 'You mustn't think your education will stop just because I'm leaving Dessau. I may have helped you to understand your lessons, but I certainly didn't give you that desire for knowledge that you seem to possess. That desire comes from God, and will remain with you whether I stay or leave.'

'It's all very well for you to say that,' muttered Moses, the tears still streaming down his face. 'But if you go to Berlin, who will teach me and explain things in a way that I can understand?'

'Perhaps, some day, when you're older, you will come to Berlin too. Then you will be able to learn about many other things – such as art, science, languages, and mathematics, as well as religion. There is so much to learn – I couldn't teach it all to you even if I stayed at the seminary. *You* must make the effort to discover things for yourself: *you* must determine to seek knowledge wherever it can be found. You must let God be your inspiration, and not let human beings dominate your life.'

Moses did his best to stop his tears. He even tried to smile. 'I wish you weren't going, even so. Nothing will be the same without you. I wish I could come to Berlin.'

'One day perhaps you will,' said Rabbi Frankel again. 'Moses, I must go. Cheer up, and may God bless you and give you courage and strength to fulfil your ambitions.'

Moses shook hands with his teacher, then waved as the coach continued on its way. He stood watching long after it had disappeared round the bend in the road, and then, slowly and reluctantly, he began walking towards the seminary.

At home, that evening, Moses was very quiet.

27

The meal his mother had prepared was scanty enough, but Moses could not manage to eat more than a couple of mouthfuls. He was so preoccupied – he scarcely seemed to hear his brothers' laughter and carefree conversation. His parents eyed each other anxiously across the table. They had noticed his red eyes and unhappy face, yet Moses' expression somehow forbade comment.

Weeks went by. Moses went just as readily to school each morning and he studied just as long and as hard each evening, yet he seemed different. His mother and father thought about things for a long time. They realised how upset Moses was at the departure of David Frankel, but they were sure that he would soon get over it. But as time went on and Moses carried on working as he always had done, but without the same enjoyment, his father decided that the time had come for him to try to influence his son's future once again.

One evening when Saul and Jente were asleep and Moses was sitting at the little table in their bedroom bent over his books and trying to decipher the words in the dim candlelight, Herr Mendel came into the room. He spoke softly to Moses, in order not to disturb the other two boys. 'Come down to my workroom. Your mother and I want to speak to you.'

With a sinking heart Moses followed his father downstairs. Without surprise he listened to the same old arguments – become a pedlar, earn some money, stop studying at school, start helping the family.

28

But the months that had gone by since Rabbi Frankel's departure had not altered Moses' resolve to become a great scholar. Perhaps, if anything, they had strengthened it. When Moses then said that he agreed it was time for him to leave the seminary, his parents thought he was at last beginning to see sense. So they could not have been less prepared for the shock their son was about to give them.

'All right, I'll leave school,' said Moses quietly, deep lines of weariness marking his forehead. 'But I still won't become a pedlar, Father. I want to go to Berlin instead. Rabbi Frankel said that when I'm older, I might be able to go – and now that I'm fourteen, I don't see why I shouldn't.'

'Moses! What are you saying?' cried his mother in horror. 'How can *you* walk the long road to Berlin. It's about eighty miles.'

'They'd never let you in even if you did get there,' almost shouted his father. He had been patient with Moses for long enough – this was too much! 'Go to bed at once and don't mention such a foolish idea to me again.'

But Moses was determined, and he steadfastly refused to change his mind. Amid the fiercest opposition from his parents and the ridicule of his brothers and his friends at the seminary, he made his plans. The next fine day, early in the morning, he was going to put his few belongings into a pack, take as much food and money as his parents could spare him, and set off on his journey.

Eighty miles was a long way, but he would walk slowly and he would get there somehow. No one took him seriously, however. His parents refused to believe he was really planning such a foolhardy trip, and his brothers roared with laughter whenever he mentioned it. Yet Moses persisted. The more people laughed or tried to persuade him not to go, the more determined he became.

When he awoke one morning, a week or so later, and saw the cloudless blue sky and could feel the crisp air that betokened a dry October day, he knew the time had come for him to leave Dessau. He dressed quietly, but Saul and Jente soon woke up. First they grumbled at Moses for disturbing them, then they teased him as he began to pack his few belongings, and finally in alarm they went to wake their parents.

An hour later Moses decided it had been the worst ordeal of his life having to say good-bye to his brothers, to his father who gave him his blessing with tears in his eyes, and to his mother who wept bitterly. He even began to wonder whether they were right – that he would suffer from exhaustion on the journey, that he would never reach Berlin, that he would never see them or anyone else again. But firmly he put these thoughts out of his mind and concentrated on the great adventure that lay ahead.

Slowly but enthusiastically Moses continued along the road that led out of Dessau and then crossed the wooden bridge that spanned the River Mulde. When he reached the other side he took one last, wistful look back at Dessau, and prayed that he would see his family again in the not too distant future.

He now began to feel a thrill of excitement. Dessau was behind him: there was no turning back. Most of the time the way to Berlin was clearly marked – coaches, horses and carts, and people trampling over the grass had made paths which could easily be followed.

Moses' main problem was money, for though his parents had given him all they could afford, it had been little enough. 'I must save some money to pay the tax when I reach Berlin,' he thought as he began working out how much, if any, could be spent on food. He had no idea what difficulties he would face – especially once he arrived in Berlin, but he knew that Jews were forced to pay taxes whenever they passed through towns and different districts – in some places the tolls were the same as those fixed for oxen!

Moses, like every other Jew, had to wear a yellow badge on his clothes to distinguish him from the Gentiles. Although the badge was intended to mark him as a member of the scorned, despised Hebrew race, Moses had been taught to regard the badge with pride. For who could be ashamed of the fact that centuries of persecution had not shaken the Jews' steadfast allegiance to their historic faith?

After a couple of hours Moses sat down to rest by the roadside. He undid his pack, and took out the loaf of bread his mother had given him. 'Blessed art Thou, O Lord our God, King of the Universe, who bringest forth bread from the earth,' said Moses thoughtfully, before taking a mouthful. Never had that blessing meant as much to him as it did now – only God knew where his next loaf of bread would come from.

Although his back was aching, Moses was determined to ignore the pain. As he rested, he considered his plans. He would walk each day for as long as he possibly could, then he would find a farm at which he could spend the night. Perhaps he might be allowed to sleep in the stables with the horses, but so long as a farmer gave him permission just to stay and sleep in a field Moses would be content.

Perhaps it was the sight of a small hunchbacked boy trudging slowly but steadily ahead, smiling at everyone, never whining nor asking for help, that made people stop to speak to him. Perhaps it was the courage that shone through the tiredness of the young Jewish boy that made people try to help him. Or perhaps it was simply the will of God that Moses' journey should be made easier – but whatever it was, Moses found that passers-by offered him food, kindly farmers' wives gave him milk, and drivers of carts let him ride along with them.

At first people shook their heads when they heard that Moses' destination was Berlin, and told him that he would never reach the city. 'You'll be all right for a while along the road in my cart,' they would say. 'You can spend the night in a barn near the farm – but what will you do when you leave me and are on your own again?'

'I'll manage somehow,' said Moses, with such conviction in his voice that no one had the heart to discourage him.

And so the journey progressed. Each night he was given a shelter over his head, each night someone would take pity on him and give him a few crusts of bread, some fruit, or some cheese. Each morning he would wake up nearer to Berlin than he had been the day before.

On the fifth day he was within walking distance of his destination. There were more signs of habitation, and the carefully cultivated green fields and rolling heath-land had given way to muddy dirt-tracks and cobbled paths, lined at intervals with small stone houses.

Moses stopped only once during that day – at an inn where he was given a drink of water and told by the well-meaning inn-keeper that Berlin was no place for a young lad like him. As Moses continued wearily on his way the afternoon sun began to disappear behind threatening black clouds. 'I must hurry,' worried Moses. 'I must get to Berlin before it's too late to find somewhere to spend the night.'

Usually he stopped to rest every hour or so, but now with Berlin so close he plodded on. He was exhausted: every step he took sent a sharp pain through his back. Hunger made him feel faint, but

33

he gritted his teeth and refused to allow himself to think.

He stopped only once – to make certain he was on the right path for the Rosenthal Gate, the only one through which Jews were allowed to enter the city. It was almost dark when he eventually drew near the low archway, with its imposing iron gate. Moses closed his eyes for a moment when he was a few steps from it—every part of his body was aching, and the gate, though so near, suddenly seemed far away.

Slowly, painfully, he put one foot in front of the other. At last he reached the gate, and he clung to it for support. He stared up at the forbidding figure of the bearded watchman standing on the other side and gasped: 'Please can I come through? I've got a little money. It's not much, but you can have it all.'

He held out his hand, offering his few *groschen*.

'Be off with you,' came the harsh retort. 'We've beggars enough in Berlin, and no more are allowed into the ghetto.'

Moses swayed. Only with a supreme effort did he stop himself from fainting. 'Oh, *please, please* let me in! I've come all the way from Dessau. I've got nowhere to go. I must get in to Berlin.'

The watchman turned the key in the lock and began walking away. 'NO MORE BEGGARS ARE COMING THROUGH THIS GATE!' he shouted back over his shoulder.

34

CHAPTER THREE

Dry Bread . . . and Books

MOSES clung motionless to the iron bars of the gate. He made no sound, his thoughts whirled in confusion as time suddenly stood still. He was aware of nothing – not even the pain in his back, nor the dreadful dilemma now facing him.

Doubtless it was this silence, instead of the expected cries of entreaty, that made the watchman turn back. He glared at the deformed figure still holding limpet-like to the gate. 'Who are you?' he growled. 'What do you want here?'

'I'm Moses Mendelssohn – from Dessau. I've come to study in Berlin.'

'What, with no money! Jewish beggars are forbidden to enter the city. You'd better come to the poor-house, and the Elders can decide what to do with you.'

Moses was horrified. He had heard about the poor-house, a building near the Rosenthal Gate where those seeking admission to the city were questioned

35

by the Jewish Elders. If they could prove their potential value to the community, they were allowed to enter the city: otherwise they were sent away with a small sum of money intended to alleviate any immediate hardship. Moses knew he would be refused admission – after all, what had he to offer? – unless Rabbi Frankel interceded for him.

'I know Rabbi Frankel,' he said hesitantly. 'I want to enrol in his classes. *He* said I should come to Berlin. . . .'

The watchman's expression changed. This was a different matter. David Frankel, Chief Rabbi of Berlin, was a personality and a power to be respected – even by the watchman at the gate. If Rabbi Frankel had told the boy to come to Berlin, then enter Berlin he must.

The watchman picked up the key which was dangling from a chain round his waist, and put it in the lock. 'Come on, then, if you're coming through,' he said surlily. 'What are you waiting for?'

Stunned from surprise and relief, Moses managed to whisper, 'Thank you, thank you.' He hurried through the gate, afraid the watchman might change his mind for the second time. 'Does Rabbi Frankel live far?'

'Up that street, left at the top, then straight on through the ghetto.'

'Thank you,' breathed Moses again as he disappeared into the darkness. Fear lent strength to his tired body. If he could not find Rabbi Frankel, if he had nowhere to spend the night, would he be turned out of the city by some other terrifying official?

Night had now fallen, and the darkness increased Moses' fear. The cold wind howled round him, and icy drops of rain began to soak through his clothes. He limped up the narrow, cobbled street, between the rows of ramshackle houses, past dark alleyways.

'Straight on, until you come to the tree, then right at the synagogue, and the house is a few doors down,' an old woman said, when Moses stammered out a request for directions.

He shivered. Never in his life had he felt as cold as he did now. His feet were numb, his lips were cracked from the cold, and his throat was parched with thirst. On he went, stumbling over the cobbles. At last he reached the house, and, with the little strength that remained within him, he banged repeatedly on the door.

Inside the house, in the back room which was warmed by a small fire, sat Rabbi Frankel with two of his pupils. They had just returned from the synagogue and were about to continue with their studies. Rabbi Frankel looked puzzled when he heard the feeble knocks at the door, and told one of his pupils to see who it was.

A few minutes later, a surprised-looking student rushed back into Rabbi Frankel's room. 'It's someone looking more dead than alive who wants to see you, sir. He says he's Moses of Dessau, and that you know him. He looks most peculiar – he's crouching in the doorway. . . .'

Rabbi Frankel stood up. In a few swift strides he was at the front door – where Moses, his face deadly white and his whole body trembling from cold and exhaustion, was half kneeling, half lying across the doorway.

'Moses!' cried the Rabbi. He held out his hand, drew the boy inside, and shut the door. He called to his pupils, and sent one of them for some dry clothes, the other for some food. He took Moses down the short passage to his work-room, and showed him to a seat by the fire. 'Don't talk,' he said, as he saw Moses attempting to speak, but no sound coming from his mouth. 'Wait until you are feeling warmer, then you can tell me what you are doing here.'

Food and warmth worked wonders, and within an hour Moses was feeling almost human again. His body still ached, his brain seemed to be spinning round, his eyes stayed open only with an effort – yet he felt content. Silently he thanked God for his safe journey, and for letting him find Rabbi Frankel so speedily.

'It was all right, except for the last two days,' explained Moses a little later. 'Luckily the weather's been good in the daytime but it's been so cold at night. I thought I would freeze yesterday evening because I couldn't find any shelter and I slept under an apple tree. All I could find to eat were blackberries, and a bruised apple which had fallen from the tree. I've spent most of my money, because whenever I came to a town, or crossed over a border, I had to pay the Jew-tax. I didn't know it would be so much, and I've only got a few *groschen* left. But I had to come, Rabbi Frankel. It was awful in Dessau after you had left, and there was no one who could teach us the way you did. My parents wanted me to become a pedlar, as they did before, so I decided to come to Berlin and study with you. I'm fourteen now, so I ought to be able to earn some money somehow.'

Rabbi Frankel thought for a moment. Although he had felt some dismay when he saw Moses at his door – he could not afford to keep the boy – he was determined to help him. He did actually need some-one to copy the Talmud for him, and Moses, with the excellent handwriting which he had learnt from his father, was just the person to do it for him. 'You can stay here for a couple of days, Moses, until we have made some arrangements. I can pay you a little if you will do some work for me, and I think one of my friends will let you stay in his house. I expect he'll give you a meal once or twice a week, and you can come here to dinner every Friday night.'

Rabbi Frankel felt more than repaid by Moses' look of gratitude. He kept his word and arranged for Moses to sleep in an attic room belonging to a good friend, who also promised to give the boy some food. And when Moses climbed the dingy, broken-down staircase to the attic a couple of days later, and surveyed the small, cobwebbed room in which he was allowed to sleep, he felt overcome with gratitude. He had never known luxury, and this room seemed to him like heaven.

He slept soundly on the straw palliasse, and when he awoke the following morning he almost burst out singing with the sheer joy of being alive in Berlin. There was a small piece of bread in his knapsack, a piece which he had been carefully hoarding until he knew he could be sure of some more food. He cut off part which had grown mouldy, and nibbled the rest, determined not to notice the peculiar dry taste.

After he had finished it, he went outside and splashed his face with water from the well, and drank from his cupped hands. Then he decided to explore. He had not yet recovered from the ordeal of his journey and found he could not walk far without resting. But this did not matter, for everything was so new to Moses and he was glad to stop and stare anyway.

He paused for a while outside the wedding-hall which was near to the synagogue, and pondered over the hardships endured by the Jews. Among the many rules imposed upon the community was one which restricted marriages. The eldest child of a family was allowed to marry and have a home of his own – provided he received official permission and could afford to pay marriage dues each year. Other children in a family could marry only if their possessions were worth a certain sum, and could afford to pay even higher marriage dues than those imposed on the eldest child. However, despite these restrictions, the Jewish population in Berlin steadily increased – much to the concern of the city officials.

The synagogue, by which Moses was now standing, had been built in 1712 and dedicated two years later. Before that, Jews were allowed to worship only in private houses. The synagogue was a plain, unpretentious building, but, as Moses discovered a little later, was beautifully decorated inside. The ceremonial objects were elaborately chased, and there were magnificent brocades hanging before the Ark. The mantles for the Scrolls of the Law had been carefully designed and painstakingly stitched with the finest thread available. The lamps hanging from the roof and the trappings for the Scrolls themselves had been worked by famous silversmiths.

Despite the unimaginative, narrow lives that Jews were expected to lead, they managed to build a community for themselves, and among the public buildings in the ghetto were a bathing-establishment, a bakery, laundry, slaughter-house, cemetery – and even a prison!

The ghetto of Berlin fascinated the young boy from Dessau and even after he had lived there for some time he still loved wandering down the narrow streets, exploring, watching passers-by, and talking eagerly to whoever ventured to speak to him.

One day, when he was walking slowly down the

41

B*

Judengasse (Jews' Street), he was so engrossed by all he saw that he never noticed two tall young men walking towards him. He craned his neck round as he passed a dark alley-way leading to a money-lender's establishment – and walked straight into the two men. He fell backwards with a bump, wincing as his body met the hard cobbles.

'That'll teach you to look where you're going,' said a laughing voice above him. 'Oh, I didn't realise you were . . . I mean, your back. . . .'

'Are you all right?' said another voice, also sounding anxious. 'We wouldn't have let you bump into us if we'd known about your back.'

Moses moved his body gingerly and was relieved to find all his limbs working – though somewhat painfully! 'I certainly *will* look where I'm going next time,' he said with a wry smile. 'I haven't always lived in Berlin, there's so much to see here, and sometimes I forget there are other people around, too!'

Moses stood up, helped by the young men, who still seemed concerned. One of them said, 'My name's Israel, and this is Aaron – Aaron Gumpertz. Just to show you how sorry we are, we'll take you to my lodgings and give you a drink and something to eat. Unless, of course, you're going somewhere else. . . .'

'No, I'm not. I'd love to come, but I haven't any money. . . .'

'Neither have I,' interrupted Israel, then he added cheerfully, 'but Aaron's family are very rich, and they keep us supplied with their left-overs.'

Eagerly Moses accompanied Aaron and Israel down the street towards the lodging-house. They were anxious to know why he was in Berlin, and whether he was a student. And over a meal of beer and boiled fish Moses heard their stories too.

He listened in horror to Israel Samosz's account of the persecution he had endured in his native Galicia. 'No one approved of my views – on religion and on life in general, nor of the way I read other books besides the Talmud – and I was forced to leave. It's wonderful to be able to study here – although, of course, we're still only supposed to concern ourselves with the Talmud, but in Berlin it's easier to get hold of other books as well! My main interest is mathematics, but I'll learn anything that's going.'

Moses turned shyly to Aaron. 'Are you studying mathematics too?'

Israel roared with laughter. 'When he adds up two and two, he makes it nine and a half! I should have explained that Aaron is the great Dr. Aaron Solomon Gumpertz – the first Jew ever to have received a doctor's degree at a Prussian university. Do you know he can tell us which is our knee and which is our elbow just by simple examination though sometimes he had to consult the diagrams in his dusty books just to make sure he hasn't got the names mixed up!'

Aaron grinned as he handed round some honey-cake. 'Now keep quiet, Israel – I can listen to you talking any time. Moses, what do you do all day?'

43

Moses explained that he had enrolled as one of Rabbi Frankel's pupils, and also helped him by copying the Jerusalem Talmud. 'I want to learn other things as well, though. Are mathematics difficult, Israel?'

'Not really. I'll give you some coaching some time, if you like. It can count as a form of penance for letting you fall over. What can you teach him, Aaron? How about some nice gruesome bloodletting, or. . . .'

'I could teach you a bit of French and English,' offered Aaron dubiously. 'I don't know if you'd be interested?'

'*Interested!*' breathed Moses, scarcely believing his ears. 'Oh, yes, I *should!*'

Israel and Aaron were as good as their word, and every day life grew more enthralling for Moses. As well as mathematics, French and English which he was learning from his friends, he continued his studies with Rabbi Frankel. In addition he was teaching himself German.

Moses had been brought up to speak Yiddish – a mediaeval dialect consisting mainly of German, but with a smattering of Hebrew – but now he was living in Berlin he wanted to be able to write and speak the pure German language. This, however, was strictly forbidden by the Jewish Elders, who felt that once people started reading about non-Jewish thoughts and beliefs they would begin to doubt the truth of what they had been taught about Judaism.

44

Nevertheless, Moses defied this strict rule and borrowed German books whenever he was able. He worked very hard, and, as the months went by, he became almost fluent in German.

All this knowledge which he was gradually acquiring helped to compensate in some measure for his lack of food. With his scanty earnings he bought a loaf of bread at the beginning of each week, then carefully cut notches into it so that he was not tempted to eat more than the day's ration. Sometimes when he went to Rabbi Frankel's home on Friday night he was so hungry that he felt almost unable to eat, yet it was this meal, and the few others which he was given regularly by the Rabbi's kindly friends, that helped to keep him alive. On the rare occasions when Moses felt depressed by his poverty he comforted himself by repeating the words of the Talmud: 'Bread with salt shalt thou eat, water by measure shalt thou drink, upon the hard earth shalt thou sleep, and a life of anxiousness shalt thou live, and labour in the study of the Law.'

Some time after his meeting with Israel and Aaron he was introduced to Abraham Kisch, a friendly and learned physician from Prague, who offered to teach him Latin. Moses never ceased to be amazed at the way his friends spent so long helping him – he didn't realise they were as much intrigued by him as he was by them. They enjoyed listening to his original and enthusiastic theories on different subjects, and they recognised in him a gifted and unusual spirit.

Ever since his first Saturday in Berlin Moses had attended Sabbath services and listened to the wise sermons of Rabbi Frankel. The thin, hunchbacked young man, following intently during the services and listening avidly to the words of the Rabbi, did not go unnoticed by the Elders of the community. Many of them spoke to him, or asked Rabbi Frankel who the boy was. Talmudic students always swelled the ranks of the congregation, yet there was something about Moses' demeanour that made him stand out among the rest.

One day, to his horror, Moses realised that he had lost one of his books – *The Merchant of Venice* by William Shakespeare. He knew that if any of the Elders found out that he had been reading the work of an Englishman he would at once be thrown out of Berlin. Moses searched frantically among the books which cluttered up his little garret, but he could not find it anywhere. He hurried round to Aaron's lodgings, where he had spent the previous evening, but there was still no sign of it.

'It must be somewhere,' said Aaron unhelpfully. 'Are you sure it isn't in your room?'

'Positive!' declared Moses, his anxiety increasing as the minutes passed. 'I read it on Saturday morning before I went to synagogue, then I realised it was getting late for the service, so I picked up my prayer-books and rushed out.'

Aaron thought for a second, then a worried expression came over his face. 'I wonder if, by mistake, you took it to synagogue with your prayer-books.'

'Oh, no!' Moses groaned. 'Surely I couldn't!'

'You'd better go and have a look: I'll come with you if you like. I only hope you didn't leave it on the floor underneath the bench!'

Anxiously the two hurried off. Aaron was by now as concerned as Moses, for it was he who had lent him the play. They reached the synagogue, and rushed up to the entrance. As they pushed open the door they almost knocked over the *shammash,* who was just coming out.

'Ah, Herr Mendelssohn!' he said as he recognised the student. 'I was coming to look for you. Herr Isaac Bernhard, who, as you know, is one of our most respected members, wishes to speak to you on an urgent and important matter. Will you go at once to his home?'

Moses and Aaron exchanged alarmed glances, and groaned in despair.

CHAPTER FOUR

Enter the Tutor

SLOWLY and sadly, Moses and Aaron walked towards the fashionable section where Isaac Bernhard lived. In a street some distance from the bustling alleys of the ghetto were some fine, detached houses belonging to the more prosperous members of the Jewish community – the merchants, craftsmen, jewellers, and others belonging to the 'Protected' class.

So far Moses had mainly come into contact with 'Tolerated' Jews – the majority of the Jewish population – who were miserably poor and were treated very harshly by the city officials. But he knew all about the Protected class, to which Isaac Bernhard belonged. Protected Jews were allowed certain privileges, and could live in their homes without fear of expulsion.

There was also a small group who were treated even better than the Protected Jews. They were the 'Court' Jews, who were under the direct protection of the Royal Court, and who could live, work and dress as they pleased. Most Courts had a Court Jew, just as they had a Court brewer, chamberlain, preacher and jester. A Court Jew had to raise money for the king, give advice on financial matters, arrange for supplies to the armies in times of war, and find jewellery, works of art or other objects to suit the whims of the monarch. Although Court Jews did not always observe their religion, they could usually be counted upon to help their fellow-Jews in times of trouble.

Moses knew that Herr Bernhard was a wealthy silk manufacturer and a power in the Jewish community, and he trembled at the thought of his forthcoming interview. He and Aaron were directed to a tall grey stone building which stood apart from the others, and, reluctantly, they made their way towards it.

They smiled wanly at each other as they parted at the gate. 'Look, perhaps you ought to tell him the book belongs to me. . . .'

'There's no point in that!' interrupted Moses. 'Why should we both be expelled from Berlin?'

'Well . . .' said Aaron, who, despite his guilt, appreciated the sense in this. 'Well . . . good luck, anyway,' he ended lamely.

'Thanks. I certainly need it!' Moses stared at the neat garden path which led to some stone steps, at the top of which was a large wooden door – the door of doom. . . .

Breathing deeply to keep up his courage, Moses

walked along that path, then up the steps. He let the large brass knocker fall, hoping against hope that no one would hear its resounding clang.

But almost immediately the door was opened by a bewigged and smartly dressed footman, and Moses was requested to step inside.

The footman, a tall, thin man, with a lined, poker-like face, said, 'Herr Bernhard is expecting you. Would you come this way, please?'

Moses took a quick look around, and gasped with astonishment. Never had he seen such a magnificent hall – the panelled walls were covered with beautiful tapestries, the floor was carpeted with an enormous Persian rug, and the crystal chandelier was glittering in the sunlight. . . .

Moses was ushered down a corridor and left standing outside a half-opened door. The footman murmured, 'Herr Bernhard is waiting for you in here,' and then discreetly disappeared.

Miserably Moses pushed open the door and stood hesitatingly on the threshold.

'Come in! Come in!' boomed a deep voice, and Moses steeled himself to look at the owner. At the far end of the room, behind a massive mahogany desk, sat a chubby little man, holding out his hand in welcome and beaming with delight at his visitor.

Moses felt he could breathe again. Perhaps this was not to be his last afternoon in Berlin after all!

He walked across the room and shook hands with Herr Bernhard, who then motioned him to a chair.

Moses gaped at the chair before settling himself upon it. He was used to hard wooden benches, not to elegant gilt chairs with seats and backs upholstered in exquisite silk! The whole room, in fact, seemed to him like another world – silk-panelled walls, a lofty ceiling, ornaments on the mantelpiece, bronze figures on marble stands . . . he scarcely knew where to look.

Herr Bernhard, although dressed in the traditional black, was unlike other men whom Moses had met. Prosperity had given him poise, confidence had given him contentment. He was a middle-aged man, with greying hair. His dark eyes twinkled and his mouth seemed ever ready to break into a smile.

'Well, Herr Mendelssohn,' he said, leaning back in his chair and looking carefully at his visitor. He seemed to like what he saw, for after a moment he said, 'I believe everyone calls you Moses, so I will do the same. Now, I've heard about you from Rabbi Frankel, who has recommended you as a tutor for my children. I am looking for someone who can teach Daniel and Joseph Hebrew and mathematics, and who will be responsible for them if my wife and I are out of town for a few days.'

Briefly Herr Bernhard explained what would be expected of the tutor: the working hours were reasonably short, and food, clothes and a small bedroom were to be included.

'I understand that you are a Hebrew scholar of some distinction,' went on Herr Bernhard, 'and are well informed about many subjects of which the authorities do not approve.'

Moses looked up quickly, but was relieved to see Herr Bernhard was smiling. 'I have studied many many things since I came to Berlin seven years ago,' he said eagerly, and then, in answer to Herr Bernhard's questions, told him how he had taught himself German, and had learned mathematics, French, English and Latin.

Bernhard was genuinely interested in this young man's zest for learning. 'What books have particularly impressed you?' he asked.

Moses replied without hesitation. 'Maimonides' *Guide to the Perplexed*. I used to study it every night when I lived with my parents in Dessau. In fact, I think it was Maimonides' fault that I've got such a hump! But still,' Moses added more seriously, 'I have the greatest admiration and respect for Maimonides, for though my body may have been weakened by the long hours of study, my soul has most certainly been strengthened. Another book I've read over and over again is . . .' and then Moses stopped.

'Out with it,' smiled Herr Bernhard. 'Do you think I don't know all about the forbidden books which you young men are daring enough to read?'

Moses relaxed. Herr Bernhard was not trying to catch him out. 'Well, it's written by an Englishman, John Locke, and is called *Essay Concerning Human Understanding*. I first came across a Latin translation of the book, and I've never got tired of reading it. In fact, I've got so interested in it that I want to read other books on philosophy, too.'

Herr Bernhard was impressed by twenty-one-year-old Moses, and did not ask him any more questions. 'I shall, of course, pay you a small salary in addition to the other amenities, and as you will be in my employment you will also be under my protection. So you need no longer be afraid of being expelled from Berlin.'

Moses' eyes shone with delight. He could have asked for no greater or more satisfying reward than this. He agreed to take up residence and start work the following week, and a few minutes later left Herr Bernhard's home in a very different frame of mind from that in which he had entered it!

And so – in 1750 – a new phase in Moses' life began. During the seven years he had lived in Berlin he had endured all manner of hardships. But now, in his new job, he was able to wear warm, untattered clothes, to eat regular and adequate meals and to live in comfort. Enthusiastically and conscientiously he set about teaching his pupils, Joseph, aged eleven, and Daniel, who was two years younger.

But when the boys were in bed Moses would spend long hours poring over his own books and pursuing his own studies. Most of his salary went on new books, and on fees for some lessons in Greek. He also continued learning mathematics, including algebra, and mercantile accounts.

Moses kept in touch with Israel and Aaron, and the

three young men met as often as they could. Their friendship remained firm, and they were always anxious to exchange news, and to pass on ideas and knowledge to each other.

Isaac Bernhard proved a very kind employer. He was always interested in his sons' lessons, and he often sat quietly in the schoolroom, listening to Moses and looking at his beautiful handwriting.

Moses, however, soon found himself faced with a problem – and that was nine-year-old Daniel. He was shy, awkward, and extraordinarily secretive. All these traits had developed since Moses' arrival, and became so pronounced that even Joseph noticed Daniel's strange behaviour.

The Bernhards were worried about this, especially as they were otherwise entirely satisfied with Moses. They talked it over with each other and then with Moses, and asked him to try to find out what was wrong. 'Daniel was always a little quieter than Joseph,' said Herr Bernhard thoughtfully, 'but now he seems worried all the time. It's not like him to behave like this – I wish you'd find out the reason, Moses.'

Moses tried several times to win Daniel's confidence. He was very patient during the lessons, and he joined in the boys' games as well as he could. But Daniel would usually break up the game soon after Moses appeared and would go off to read or sit by himself in his bedroom.

One week-end, Herr and Frau Bernhard decided

to visit some friends who lived a short distance from Berlin. They left the boys in Moses' care, telling him that they had complete confidence in his ability to keep them happy and free from harm.

The Bernhards left home on Friday morning. Moses gave his usual lessons to Joseph and Daniel, and took them to synagogue for the early evening service. When they were safely home and in bed Moses went to his own room and began reading.

An hour or so later the door suddenly burst open and Joseph, his brown hair tousled, and his nightwear dishevelled, rushed in. 'Daniel has disappeared,' he cried, surprise and alarm in his voice. 'I don't know what's happened to him.'

Moses felt his whole body go cold. Daniel . . . disappeared . . . could he have been kidnapped? Could some bandit have enticed the boy away, intending to hold him for ransom? He tried to keep the fear out of his voice as he said, 'You must be wrong, Joseph. He is probably in the house somewhere.'

'He's not! I've looked everywhere, and none of the servants have seen him.'

Moses stood up and took his cloak which was lying over a chair. 'Where can he be? Why has he gone?'

'I've no idea!' said Joseph, answering both questions at once. Then he thought for a moment. 'Perhaps he's gone to the woods. Once or twice I've seen him walking towards them, but when I've said

I'd come with him, he's insisted that we both walk home instead. He really was mysterious. I thought he was trying to hide something under his cloak, but he swore he wasn't and made a terrific fuss when I tried to look.'

Joseph was almost as worried as Moses. He was fond of his young brother, and had been puzzled by his strange behaviour.

Moses thought quickly. 'Do you mean the woods at the far end of this street?'

'Yes,' said Joseph. 'Shall I come with you?'

'No. You'd better go to bed, but I'll come and see you as soon as I get back. Don't worry about Daniel. He can't be far away.'

Before Joseph had time to protest Moses was hurrying down the stairs. He rushed across the hall and out through the front door.

Once outside, he walked swiftly towards the near-by woods, his mind in a turmoil. Whatever had possessed Daniel to leave home at dead of night . . . and wander off in the moonlight? Was the boy mad – or merely mischievous?

Moses had now reached the edge of the woods. The tall fir trees looked eerie and unwelcoming, and Moses wondered whether Daniel had panicked if he had wandered far into the ghostly woods.

Moses' head was throbbing painfully. What would he do if Daniel could not be found? As he hurried along the path, he glanced anxiously around, but could see no trace of the boy.

Then he came to a clearing, and almost collapsed from sheer relief. There, crouching on the ground, burrowing in the soil, was the small, slim figure of Daniel.

'Daniel,' said Moses sternly.

The boy, startled, spun round so quickly that he almost overbalanced. 'Oh . . .' he said feebly, confusion and anxiety in his voice.

Moses walked forward. He dug his heel into the ground, and started moving the soil which Daniel had been trying to smooth over. His shoe came in contact with something. He stooped down, and picked up a book. Then he gasped. It was the copy of *The Merchant of Venice* that he had searched for so frantically the day he had been summoned to Herr Bernhard's house – and had eventually given up as lost!

He said nothing. He just stared at Daniel, waiting for an explanation.

Daniel looked sullen. 'Well, I found it ages ago in synagogue. I'd stayed behind to look for a ball that I'd taken to synagogue, but which dropped out of my hand and rolled under the benches during the service. The book was lying on the floor, near my ball, and I took it home with me. At lunch that day I asked Father whether he would like to read a book which didn't seem like a Hebrew book, and he said that whoever was found with that sort of book would be thrown out of the city.' Daniel's voice broke, and he seemed to be fighting back tears.

'But I don't understand,' said Moses gently. 'Why didn't you tell him that you had picked it up in synagogue?'

'Well, I would have done, but we started talking about something else and I forgot. A few days later we heard that you were going to be our tutor. I remembered the book soon after you'd arrived, and one night I looked at the book again and saw some handwritten notes. The writing was *exactly* the same as yours. I've been hiding the book ever since, waiting for a chance to bury it in the woods where no one can find it. I think that's the safest place for it, don't you?'

Daniel looked at Moses, his face full of concern. He was a kind-hearted boy, and felt appalled at the idea of anyone – especially someone he knew – being made to leave the city.

'Is that why you've been behaving so strangely?' Daniel nodded.

Moses put his arm round the young boy's shoulders. 'It was very kind of you to try to hide the book for me, and I'm sorry you've been worried about it. But your father does know I read foreign books, and he doesn't seem to mind. So I think we'll take *The Merchant of Venice* home with us again.' Moses lovingly fingered the battered copy. How relieved Aaron would be, too!

Moses was touched that Daniel should have gone to such lengths to protect him from trouble. When the Bernhards arrived home the following day, he

58

told them the whole story, and they were very glad to know that the problem of Daniel was now solved.

During the next four years Moses did his best to teach Joseph and Daniel as much as they could absorb. But though he liked his job, he was secretly just as pleased as his pupils when the lessons for the day were over. Then he could escape to his room and bury his head in his books. For hours and hours he would read undisturbed, and sometimes he would try to write essays on philosophy, which had now become his favourite subject.

But happy though he was, he at times had moments of uneasiness. Joseph and Daniel were growing up. Soon they would start to learn a trade, and would need their tutor no longer.

Moses wondered what would happen to him then. Would fortune continue to shine on him, or would he be forced back into the narrow life of the ghetto?

CHAPTER FIVE

Early Success

MOSES did his best to forget his troubles, but the harder he tried the more difficult it became. Daniel and Joseph were both longing for the time when they could be free from their lessons, and they pestered their father to let them work in his factory. But Herr Bernhard insisted that they should complete their education before they learned a trade. They then began to resent having a tutor. Moses, who had always considered himself placid, now discovered he had a temper, and their lessons frequently dissolved into shouting matches. Soon he was feeling thoroughly tired of his life at the Bernhards.

He consoled himself by taking a tremendous interest in a magazine to which a friend suggested he should contribute. He wrote articles on natural history, which he based on sayings from the Talmud and other rabbinic writings.

But his satisfaction with his new work was short-lived. He was strolling down the street one day past

the synagogue when an elderly, grey-bearded gentle-
man stopped him. Moses was puzzled for a moment,
then he recognised the two other men with him.
These three were among the Elders of the congregation, and their word was law on all religious matters.

'We have seen the latest number of your magazine,
Herr Mendelssohn,' said the grey-haired man, Herr
Samuel. 'We are disgusted that you should write such
articles. We are horrified that you have wasted the
time which you could have usefully employed in your
Talmudic studies by writing these things.'

Moses looked indignant. He had had a difficult
morning with Daniel and Joseph, and now he was
spoiling for a fight. 'What's wrong with them?' he demanded indignantly.

'*Everything!*'

'Utterly disgraceful!'

'How *dare* you question us!'

Moses was taken aback. The vehemence of the
chorus of replies made him hesitate. 'I just wanted to
know!' he said, trying not to sound as rude as he felt.

Herr Samuel appointed himself the spokesman of
the trio. In no uncertain terms he told Moses that the
articles were obviously intended to incite people to
revolt against Talmudic teachings. He was to cease
writing them forthwith. Moses was to confine his
activities to the accepted forms of religious study.
'Our influence in this community – even with Herr
Bernhard – is considerable,' went on Herr Samuel. 'If
you wish to continue living in Berlin, you must

abide by our decision.' And on this ominous note Herr Samuel ended his lecture. The three men strode past Moses, who stood glaring angrily at their departing figures.

'How intolerant and ridiculous they are!' declared Moses aloud.

'Who?' said a voice behind him.

Moses spun round. Aaron Gumpertz was standing a few yards away and was regarding him quizzically. 'I saw you chatting to Herr Samuel and his friends – or should I say *your* friends, now?' Aaron asked jokingly.

Moses grimaced. 'Certainly not!' he said, and then told Aaron about the conversation. Aaron's annoyance almost equalled his own, and Moses felt slightly consoled by his friend's sympathy.

'They said that Jews should only write and think about religion, but really they don't want people to think at all,' Moses said somewhat bitterly. 'It's so stupid – we're just supposed to believe what we are told, and never to ask *why*.'

'*You* do!'

'And so do you!' retorted Moses. 'The trouble is that we study these Talmudic teachings, but we are not supposed to develop any of the thoughts and ideas which the rabbis have expressed. But time doesn't stand still, so why should our minds?'

Aaron thought for a moment. 'They don't really stand still. Look at the books we read. We're always learning something new.'

'Well, perhaps you are,' said Moses gloomily, 'but I'm not. I've studied so many things in general, but none in particular. I haven't got a complete grasp and understanding of any one subject. I suppose that's the result of learning more or less by myself. You and Israel have helped me a lot – and I wouldn't know as much as I do if you hadn't spent so much of your time teaching me. But I feel now that I want to meet someone who could help me solve definite problems – who has, perhaps, written about controversial matters and has reached some sane and satisfactory conclusion.'

'You ought to talk to Gotthold Lessing,' declared Aaron after thinking for a moment. 'Isaac Hess and I are playing chess to-morrow evening, and Lessing's bound to be there, too. Come along, and we'll introduce you.'

Moses accepted this invitation at once. His depression disappeared, and excitement took its place. Gotthold Lessing was a well-educated and liberal-minded Christian journalist and man of letters, who had caused a great stir with his play *The Jews*, which had appeared five years ago. This was about a Jew who rescued a nobleman from two murderous rogues. As a token of gratitude, the nobleman proffered the hand of his daughter in marriage. When the Jew declared his religion, the offer was at once withdrawn, though the nobleman deigned to remark, 'How estimable the Jews would be if they were all like you!' The Jew retorted, 'How amiable the

63

Christians would be if they all had your fine qualities!'

This tolerant attitude towards the Jews offended many Christians, to whom the portrayal of a Jew as the hero instead of the villain of the piece was a revolutionary idea! But Lessing ignored the criticism and abuse from his co-religionists. He judged people as he found them, and when he decided the picture that many Christians painted of the Jews was a false one, he did not hesitate to say so.

Lessing's sense of justice annoyed most of his Christian colleagues, who had severely censured him on a previous occasion when he began mixing and making friends with a crowd of actors. But Lessing had just laughed at them, and proceeded to do exactly as he wished.

Moses and Aaron arranged to meet next day, and promptly at nine o'clock the following evening Moses eagerly followed Aaron and Isaac down some stone steps into a crowded, smoky basement room. There, young men were sitting opposite each other, leaning forward with their elbows on the wooden table as they concentrated on the chess-board between them.

The tables were divided by low wooden partitions, and small boys darted in and out carrying tankards of beer and platters piled with bread, cold meats of all kinds, and dried fruits. A genial old man, dressed from head to foot in sombre grey, acted as host. It was his job to show newcomers to vacant seats, and to satisfy the wants of all the club members.

He came over to Aaron and greeted him like an old friend. Aaron explained that he wanted to introduce Moses to Lessing, and then glanced swiftly round the room, his eyes growing accustomed to the dim light. There was a slight murmur of conversation and some laughter from a corner as two of the players exchanged a private joke. 'The one nearest to us is Gotthold Lessing,' said Aaron to Moses and made his way over to him.

Lessing, whose fair hair was waved and peri-wigged and tied with a bow at the nape of his neck, looked up as Moses approached with Isaac and Aaron. He wore a velvet jacket and a white lace cravat over his high-buttoned waistcoat. Even in the flickering candlelight Moses was conscious of Lessing's eyes, large, slightly bulbous, but friendly and enquiring.

'Hello,' he said, raising his hand in friendly salute. 'I'm glad you've come to interrupt us. My knights and my bishops are in league against me – I'm sure Stephen's arranged this conspiracy!'

They all laughed. 'Come and join us,' said Lessing, moving back from the table and making room for the others. 'You don't mind, do you, Stephen? Your victory's certain now.'

Isaac introduced Moses, and then he and Aaron started talking to Stephen. Moses and Gotthold Lessing surveyed each other intently, then, simultaneously, they smiled. And in that moment the seeds

65

c

of a lasting friendship were sown, a friendship that was to have a profound effect on both their lives.

'I've wanted to meet you for a long time,' said Moses shyly. Talking to strangers was still something of an ordeal for him.

'And I'm delighted to meet you,' replied Lessing, and then the two entered into conversation. They talked first about chess, then about Lessing's present work, then about Moses' life in Berlin. They were still hard at it long after the others had gone, and the club's host was sitting sleepily in the corner waiting for the two men to leave so he could himself retire to bed.

Inevitably their conversation turned to Lessing's outspoken and courageous play, *The Jews*. 'You remind me of my hero,' said Lessing, though more to himself than to Moses. He was sure he would find in Moses the noble qualities which he had attributed to the Jew in his play, and was delighted that his convictions were not unjustified.

In the small hours of the morning they parted. They met, however, the following day, and almost every day after that. As their friendship developed, Moses was delighted to find his general knowledge greatly increased. Lessing, for his part, was amazed at Moses' grasp of languages, mathematics, philosophy and poetry – especially as Moses was mainly self-taught.

One day they were discussing the famous philosophers Spinoza and Leibnitz. When Moses expressed his admiration for the different points of view of these two men, Lessing had his great idea. 'You ought to write some conversations between them,' he suggested. 'Your German's good enough.'

Moses liked this idea, and began work almost at once. He spent considerable time re-reading the works of the two men, and then started writing his *Philosophical Dialogues*. As Joseph and Daniel frequently spent the day with their father in his factory, he found he could work for hours quite undisturbed.

It was now the year 1754, and Moses was still the paid employee of Isaac Bernhard. He knew he could not allow this state of affairs to continue, so, one morning, with the greatest reluctance, he went down to Herr Bernhard's room and asked him if he could spare a few minutes.

Herr Bernhard readily agreed. 'In fact,' he said, 'I was just about to send for you, Moses, as there is something that we must discuss.'

Moses swallowed uncomfortably. He thought he should make things easier for Herr Bernhard so he said, 'It is time that I left your employment, sir.'

'Indeed!' Herr Bernhard raised his eyebrows enquiringly.

'Er . . . yes . . .' said Moses awkwardly. 'I . . . shall carry on with my studies at . . .' He stopped, not knowing what to say next.

'So you wish to leave?'

'No, I mean, yes.'

Herr Bernhard leaned back in his chair and laughed. 'Moses, you look as though your last hour has come! What is the trouble? You remind me of the time when you came to see me four years ago, terrified in case you were to be expelled from the city. If you have made up your mind to leave, I certainly shall not stand in your way. But I should be very reluctant to see you go, as I would like you to become a book-keeper in my silk factory. Your excellent handwriting and your outstanding mathematical ability will be great assets. Do you want to change your mind, or do you still wish to work elsewhere?'

'No! I mean . . .' Moses, confused, scarcely knew what he was saying. 'I mean, yes, I should like to change my mind, and no, I don't want to work elsewhere.'

'Then that's settled. You know the way to the factory. Please be there to-morrow morning at seven o'clock.'

Moses was delighted. Irksome though the work would probably be, he could still live in security with the Bernhards, and in the evenings there would doubtless be time for him to continue his own writing and studying.

A few days later he met Lessing and told him his news. Lessing was almost as pleased as Moses that he could remain in Berlin unfettered by financial worries. 'We must celebrate!' cried Lessing. 'But first, tell me how the *Philosophical Dialogues* are getting on.'

Moses shyly handed his friend a wad of parchment which he had been carrying beneath his cloak. 'I've finished them. I don't suppose they're much good, but I've done my best. Are you sure you want to be bothered reading them?'

'Of course. I'll have a look at them to-night. Let's go now to the coffee-house and tell the others about your new job! You might even get some orders – or will you present us all with silk cravats?'

'Not likely,' grinned Moses. 'I'm in charge of the accounts, not the stock.'

'How ungenerous!' declared Lessing in mock indignation. 'But I suppose next time we meet you'll be dressed in silk, anyway.'

Laughing and joking, they set off for the coffee-house, to which Moses had also become a frequent visitor.

Among the members of the coffee-house at that time was a young bookseller, Christopher Frederic Nicolai, and Lessing and Moses felt themselves drawn towards him. The three soon became friends, and spent much of their free time together. Nicolai and Moses found they had a lot in common, for both were mainly self-taught, neither had been to university and both were business-men. Nicolai often spent an hour of two helping Moses with his study of modern languages, and he persuaded him to continue learning Greek.

Moses was now accepted by most of Lessing's Christian contemporaries, whose admiration of intellect overcame their religious prejudices. His personality, his conversation and his understanding won him many friends, and people no longer wondered why Lessing was so frequently in the company of the hunchbacked Jew.

Life had certainly changed for Moses since that day – twelve years ago – when he had first sought admission to Berlin. Since that time he had studied hard and taken advantage of every facility offered to him. Now he felt comparatively secure : his future with Herr Bernhard seemed assured and life appeared full of exciting prospects.

To his surprise, as the months went by, Lessing never mentioned his *Philosophical Dialogues*. Moses was sure he must have read them, but felt too shy to ask him. Eventually he brought up the subject, and was both hurt and astonished when Lessing said he had not yet had time to study them.

'If you're too busy, I might as well take the manuscript home with me,' said Moses. As he had written them on Lessing's suggestion, he thought his friend should have read them by now.

'I've been working hard,' replied Lessing, with a slight smile, 'but I intend to read them to-night. But stay and have some supper with me first.'

'No, thank you, I can't.' Moses felt annoyed that Lessing had treated the subject of his essays so casually, but also felt discouraged. Perhaps they weren't any good, and Lessing didn't know how to tell him.

'Have you bought any new books?' Lessing asked suddenly.

'Not for a few weeks. I like to send money to my parents in Dessau as often as I can, but I spend what's left on books. I must save up now for a new cloak: this one is so thin that it hardly protects me at all.'

'Well, this ought to help towards it.' Lessing fumbled among some papers on his table, and handed over some money. 'I thought you'd accept whatever the publishers offered you.'

Moses blinked in astonishment. 'What are you talking about?'

'Oh, and this goes with it.' Lessing handed Moses a small volume. 'You'll probably want to read it to-night, too.'

Moses stared at the book, then his eyes almost popped out of his head. He opened the cover – the author was anonymous, but the title was *Philosophical Dialogues*!

CHAPTER SIX

A Royal Summons

THE *Philosophical Dialogues* were published in 1755 and were greeted with excitement and interest. This encouraged Moses so much that he decided to continue writing in the German language. As time went by, he had other essays published, and his work began to command respect. He now had more self-confidence, and though his manner was as mild as ever he began to develop an obstinate streak. He would listen politely to well-meaning advice, but unless he whole-heartedly agreed with it he would proceed to do the opposite.

After he had passed the age of twenty-five he found that fathers of young daughters were taking an interest in him. But if anyone mentioned the word 'marriage' to him he instantly changed the subject. First of all, he was positive that no good-looking girl would want to marry a hunchback; and secondly he was quite satisfied with his life and had no intention of letting anyone share it.

72

Only with Lessing did he discuss the subject. Perhaps one day he would settle down, but he was far too busy to consider it now! Lessing would laugh at him, tell him he should be flattered, and remind him of the words of the Talmud : 'He who weds a good woman, it is as if he had fulfilled all the precepts of the Law.'

One evening, when they were talking together in a beer cellar, Lessing asked Moses if he were still frittering away his spare time with prospective fathers-in-law.

Moses looked at him in exasperation and did not deign to reply.

'I only mentioned it,' said Lessing with a smile, 'because I wondered if you were too busy to help me produce a magazine.'

It was obvious from Moses' expression that he was not too busy, so Lessing immediately told him more about it. The main idea of the magazine would be to criticise newly-published works of literature, and the two friends eagerly spent the rest of the evening making plans for the first issue.

The full title of the magazine was *Letters Concerning Recent German Literature,* though Moses and Lessing referred to it in German simply as *Literaturbriefe.* To their delight the magazine was well received, and gradually it was expanded so as to include discussions on art and science as well as literature. Several of their friends contributed to it, although the bulk of the work was still done by Lessing and Moses.

C*

One morning, in 1760, Lessing handed Moses a volume of French poems which had just been published. 'They're by King Frederick, so you'd better review it politely.'

Moses flicked through the first few pages, then he murmured thoughtfully, '*Why* should we review it politely? All the time we've been producing *Literaturbriefe* we've made a point of being completely impartial. . . .'

'Don't be ridiculous!' interrupted Lessing. 'You know quite well that the King thinks everything he writes or says or does is wonderful, and he expects his subjects to share his high opinion of himself. Just for once, you can be appreciative rather than truthful.'

'No, I *can't!*' retorted Moses, then, seeing Lessing's horrified expression, he added, 'Well, perhaps it'll be better than his usual work.'

Lessing decided not to pursue the matter. He was positive that Moses didn't really intend to criticise King Frederick's poems. No one would be so foolish!

Moses read the poems carefully, then he spent a lot of time and trouble on his review. At last he was satisfied with what he had written.

When the next issue of *Literaturbriefe* appeared it was welcomed with its normal amount of interest. The usual number of copies was circulated, but then there suddenly came a demand for more. Everyone wanted to read it.

Moses' criticism of the French poems was causing many eyebrows to be raised in astonishment, and many heads to be shaken in alarm. For the Jewish philosopher had actually been daring enough to find fault with the monarch's work! It was true that he had praised it, but at the same time he had said that it was a pity that the King had made himself acquainted with French at the expense of the German language! The King of Prussia made no secret of his admiration for the French language and literature, and his scorn for the German. Moses had always thought this was wrong, and he was glad that his review had given him the excuse for saying so publicly.

Lessing was secretly alarmed at the things his friend had written, though he had to admit that there were compliments as well as criticism. 'Are you looking for trouble?' he demanded crossly, when he first saw the review.

Moses shrugged his shoulders carelessly. 'For goodness sake, stop fussing. The King will notice only my admiring words – he won't see what I'm getting at!'

That, as it turned out, was perfectly true. A copy of *Literaturbriefe* was taken one Sunday morning into the Royal Library at the Castle in Potsdam, and was handed to King Frederick the Great of Prussia by one of his more intelligent courtiers. The King read the review, satisfied at the fulsome praise. Then he laid it aside, and would have forgotten it completely had not the courtier murmured, 'Your Majesty has no doubt noticed the veiled insults in this article.'

King Frederick looked up in astonishment. He demanded to know what the courtier meant, and, as he listened, his eyes narrowed and his pink face turned almost purple. . . .

Two weeks had now gone by since *Literaturbriefe* had been published. There had been no sign of displeasure from the Palace, and Lessing had many times sighed with relief. Now they were both thinking about and planning the next issue.

On Sunday afternoon Moses and Lessing decided to stroll through the Rosenthal Gate and explore the countryside round the city. Moses couldn't go too far because of his hump-back, but he always enjoyed walking through the fields, especially as Lessing was quite willing to rest beneath the shady trees. Nor did they waste their time, for they would talk about *Literaturbriefe* and decide which of the newly published works they should each review.

That day they found a secluded spot on the river bank, and, though they started off by working hard, they somehow found the gently flowing water and the soft warmth of the sun lulling them to sleep.

Suddenly they both sat upright in alarm. They heard a shout, then, before they had quite realised what had happened, someone had fallen headlong over their legs.

'Joseph!' said Moses in amazement.

Joseph Bernhard smiled ruefully, and rubbed his bruised knees. 'Well, I'm glad I've found you anyway . . . but I wish I'd seen you before I fell on you.'

'So do we!' retorted Moses. 'What on earth do you want? Have you been looking for me?'

Joseph nodded. 'For about two hours! This letter was brought to the house, and Father told me to find you right away.' He then handed over a large folded document.

Hurriedly Moses broke the seal and opened the paper. After a moment he gave a whistle of surprise, and handed the document to Lessing.

'A royal summons!' groaned Lessing. 'You've got to present yourself at the Palace of Sans Souci for an audience with His Majesty. So the worst has happened!'

Moses was looking indignant rather than dismayed. 'Look when I have to attend. Next Saturday! Why couldn't he have chosen another day? Why did it have to be the Sabbath?'

Lessing shrugged his shoulders. 'You asked for trouble when you wrote your review,' he told him bluntly. 'Heaven knows what will happen to you now!'

As he stared at the forbidding words on the parchment Moses wondered whether he had gone too far. But he pretended not to care, and Lessing marvelled at his cheerful mood.

However, Moses had many anxious moments as the next few days went by. He left Berlin early on Friday so as to arrive at Potsdam before Sabbath, and he spent a sleepless night at a little inn in the

town. Next day, with his head held high, he marched
through the streets to King Frederick's summer
palace. He showed the royal summons to the uni-
formed guard at the gate, who allowed him to pass
through into the grounds.

Moses felt his courage desert him as he walked
slowly along the wide carriageway leading to the
palace. He found himself trembling, but he tried to
control his fear by concentrating on his surroundings.
Even in his anxiety he was vaguely aware of the
marble statues, and, as he drew nearer to the palace,
the magnificent terraces and a pond with fountains
playing. Herr Bernhard had told him there was even
a Chinese pavilion and a Greek temple within the
park, but Moses did not feel in the least like sight-
seeing then!

At last he reached the castle – and the forbidding
figures of the King's Hussars, the favoured regiment
which guarded the royal residence. Again he presented the summons, which was carefully scrutinized,
and then he was ordered to enter the castle by a door
at the rear, to which he was escorted by two of the
soldiers.

Moses was shown into a small room, and then was
left alone. Fearfully he waited.

After twenty minutes the door was opened and two
bewigged and liveried footmen bade him follow
them. As he was taken along a wide marble corridor
Moses caught a glimpse of the dining-room, and
gaped at the magnificent gilded bronze ornaments on

the white panelled walls. Another room which he glanced at was the music room, famed for its splendid Chinese paintings.

But he had no time to stop and stare. On he hurried, trying to keep up with the footmen, past the salon, the robing-room, the audience room . . . until they reached the library. Waiting outside was one of the royal officials, who gazed scornfully at Moses as he approached. Then, with a flourish, the footmen opened the double doors of the library, and the official hissed to Moses to step inside.

The library was a small round room with a high roof. Its walls were of cedar wood, and bookcases alternated with mirrors, windows and a fireplace. There was a large desk in the centre of the room, and Moses found himself bowing low before the hostile gaze of the monarch.

King Frederick was a small, distinguished-looking man, with prominent blue eyes and, when he chose, an agreeable expression. He was a good talker, but a bad listener, and he was very contemptuous of other people – unless, of course, they belonged to the intellectual class. The King, who was forty-eight, greatly respected intellect, and for several years had had the famous French philosopher Voltaire staying with him at Sans Souci.

Moses raised his head and stared at the King, who at once picked up the copy of *Literaturbriefe*, crumpled it up, and flung it at Moses' feet. Rising from his chair, he shouted angrily, 'On what grounds do you, a lowly Jew, dare to set yourself up as a critic? I am the King of Prussia! You are a mere servant! I have the finest brain in the land, and my verses are read and admired by the greatest of French scholars. Yet, *you* . . .' At this point King Frederick was spluttering to such an extent that he had to pause to draw breath.

Moses swallowed. King Frederick's fiery temper and intolerance were well known. He dreaded to think what punishment lay in store for him. He opened his mouth to speak, unhappily aware of the mocking smile of one of the officials who was standing behind the King. For a moment no words came, then he managed to stammer out, 'A maker of verses plays at ninepins; and one who plays at ninepins, be he king or peasant, must abide by the decision of the marker on the result of his bowling.'

Suddenly the King's wrath subsided. He could see that this insignificant Jew was, after all, no fool . . . and also he was no coward. He sat down in his chair, and nodded his head at Moses. The reply had taken him by surprise. He had expected excuses, cringing apologies, pleas for mercy – but certainly not a reasonable answer to his question!

And then King Frederick remembered a phrase in Moses' review that had pleased him. Moses had spoken of the King's clever choice of words, and in this, he had said, there were few his equal. By a curious coincidence Moses suddenly remembered it too, and, raising his eyes from the floor, he repeated this very compliment. King Frederick nodded in agreement, and then launched into a hymn of praise for his own work.

When he had finished speaking, he waved his hand towards the doors, and Moses rightly took this as a sign of dismissal. He bowed low before the King again and then thankfully took leave of the royal presence.

Moses hurried from the palace grounds, and, without even stopping on the way for refreshment, he began the journey back to Berlin. He was thankful to have been let off so lightly, and he felt he never wanted to see Potsdam again.

'Next time I shall listen to Lessing's advice,' vowed Moses to himself, regretting his earlier stubbornness. 'I never want to conflict with authority again.'

But immediately afterwards he wondered whether he would always keep that vow!

CHAPTER SEVEN

Love Looks In

THE story of Moses' visit to the King spread quickly through Berlin. Moses himself said little about it, but the Marquis d'Argens, a royal courtier who was present at the meeting, described the scene to all his friends. The Marquis was full of admiration for Moses' courage, and soon afterwards called on him at Herr Bernhard's home. He told Moses that he would be proud to be numbered among his friends, and after Moses had recovered from the surprise, not only of being visited by a royal courtier, but also of hearing this astonishing statement, he happily entertained him for the rest of the afternoon in his room. After that, they often met, and the Marquis found Moses and his friends a refreshing change from the pomp and insincerity of the royal Court.

Moses now began to find that his hard work and his knowledge of philosophy were slowly being recognised. He was invited to join a 'Coffee-house of the Learned', a select society whose membership was to be limited to about a hundred scientists. Moses was delighted at this honour, but he felt very worried at the thought of lecturing once a month on a scientific subject, which all members had to do. When his turn came round, he persuaded a friend to read his essay – which he called *Inquiry into Probability* – but he was recognised as the author and loudly applauded. After that, he felt more confident, and managed to give the following lectures himself.

In 1760, to Moses' great disappointment, Lessing left Berlin to take up a job in Breslau. Both hated the idea of separation, for their friendship had deepened as the years had passed, and they had been drawn even more closely together, their lively wit and intellect complementing each others.

Moses felt lost without his friend, and time began to hang heavily on his hands. One day, when he was reading the Midrash, he came across these words by Rabbi Jacob: 'He who has no wife lives without good, or help, or joy, or blessing, or atonement.'

This made him stop and wonder. Perhaps he ought to find himself a wife.

Soon afterwards a friend told him about a pretty blue-eyed girl called Fromet Gugenheim, who lived in Hamburg and who admired his books. Moses was assured that her father, Abraham Gugenheim, a trader, would be delighted to welcome him to his house at any time that Moses happened to be in Hamburg.

'Why don't you go and meet her, anyway?' suggested the friend. 'I've known her father for many years, and I think you would like his daughter. It's time you settled down, Moses. You're thirty-two years old – and if you don't marry soon you never will!'

Moses took Herr Gugenheim's address, and promised to call on him. He made arrangements to leave Berlin for a short time, and a few days later – in April, 1761 – he found himself in Hamburg. He made his way at once to the merchant's house and was greeted very cordially by Herr Gugenheim. He was a soft-spoken, kindly man, who lived modestly in a small house near the centre of the city. His home was clean and comfortable, but contained no luxuries. He made enough money to be able to feed and clothe his wife and family, and to satisfy his own needs. More than that he did not want, for he believed that worldly goods were not a sign of happiness.

He took Moses to his work-room, and Frau Gugenheim came in with some wine and cake. The two men sat talking for a while, and then Herr Gugenheim went upstairs to fetch his daughter. Fromet, who was dressed in a simple, blue gown, entered the room somewhat hesitantly, and stood shyly by the door as Moses rose from his chair and bowed. Almost immediately Herr Gugenheim left them alone, and Moses did his best to break the atmosphere of embarrassment that had overcome them. 'I was told that you have read my books,' he said smilingly to the prim-looking, golden-haired girl. 'Did you find them very boring?'

Fromet looked at him quickly, startled by the question. Then she smiled too. 'No, of course not,' she answered quietly. 'I couldn't understand them all, but I liked reading them.'

They talked for a while – at least Moses talked and Fromet listened. Each was busy summing up the other, for their lifetime's happiness might depend upon this meeting.

Moses felt drawn towards the slim, gentle Fromet. He admired her soft, pink cheeks, her golden hair, and her demure expression, and he decided then and there that she should be his wife.

Soon Herr Gugenheim returned. They talked for a few moments longer and then Moses said, 'I must go now, but may I come again to-morrow?'

'By all means,' replied Herr Gugenheim. 'We shall be delighted to see you.'

With a light heart and a sense of happiness Moses left the Gugenheim home. He was not deeply in love with Fromet – how could he be after such a short time? – but she seemed to him to be good and kind – and very attractive as well. He went straight to the lodgings which Herr Gugenheim had recommended and settled himself in. The evening passed slowly and Moses found he could hardly wait for the following day when he would be able to see Fromet again.

Next morning he went eagerly to her home and, as

before, was taken by Herr Gugenheim to the work-room. Almost before they had sat down, Moses said, 'Herr Gugenheim, I should like to marry your daughter if you will grant me permission. I would do all I could to make her happy and I. . . .'

'Herr Mendelssohn, I do not quite know how to tell you. . . .'

The excitement went from Moses' face. Only then did he become aware of Herr Gugenheim's manner – embarrassed and upset. 'Is something wrong?' he asked anxiously. 'Have you changed your mind about me?'

'No, no, it isn't I who have changed my mind. But . . . well. . . .'

'Then is it Fromet?'

Herr Gugenheim did not meet Moses' puzzled gaze. Staring awkwardly at the ground, he said, 'Er . . . I should be more than pleased, but . . . er . . . my daughter. . . .'

'Fromet doesn't want to marry me. I suppose I'm not much of a proposition – with a stammer and a hump . . .' mused Moses sadly, but not bitterly. 'Oh, well . . .' he shrugged his shoulders and tried to smile.

Herr Gugenheim did not know what to say to soften the blow. He was, in fact, almost as disappointed as Moses, for he was certain that Fromet would have found happiness with such a man. 'I'm very sorry, Moses. I should have been very glad if Fromet had consented to be your bride, but she has

made up her mind and will not be influenced by anything that I say.'

In allowing his daughter to decide, Herr Gugenheim was defying the custom of the time. It was usual
for a father to choose a suitor and make all the
arrangements for the marriage – without considering
the feelings of the prospective bride.

'May I see her again? Just to say good-bye.'

'Certainly,' replied Herr Gugenheim in a relieved
tone. He was glad Moses was taking it so well, and
admired him for trying to hide his disappointment.

Moses was shown upstairs to a small room where
Fromet was sitting by the window intent upon her
needlework. She looked startled when her father
appeared, followed by her would-be suitor, then embarrassed as her father left the room. She bent her
head over her tapestry, and blushed when Moses said,
'Your father has told me how you feel about me, and
I can quite understand that a short, unprepossessing
hunchback doesn't fit your dreams of a husband.'

Fromet coloured even more deeply, and a tear slid
down her cheek and dropped on to her needlework.
She was a kind-hearted girl, and though she was determined not to marry Moses she hated to hurt his
feelings.

Moses felt a faint hope stir within him. If Fromet
cared enough to shed even a single tear, perhaps he
still had a chance. 'I've only come to say good-bye to
you. I'm going back to Berlin this afternoon. There's
so much work for me to do there, and I've started

writing an essay – on philosophy, of course – that I want to finish as soon as I can.'

Moses went on talking, and Fromet sat quietly listening. 'How wonderfully he explains things,' she thought to herself. 'No one else has ever talked to me like this before . . . but I couldn't possibly spend the rest of my life with a man who is so unattractive!'

Slowly and adroitly Moses changed the conversation from philosophy to the subject of love. He discussed it impersonally, of course, and at first Fromet did not realise how his remarks affected them. Almost against her will she found herself fascinated by what he was saying.

'I believe marriages are made in heaven,' declared Moses, 'and we poor mortals have nothing to do with it.'

'Do you *really* think so?' Fromet was intrigued by this romantic idea. She'd always believed that marriages were supposed to be made by fathers!

'I certainly do,' said Moses with a smile, and his heart warmed towards the shy, fair-haired girl sitting facing him. How he wished she would reciprocate his affection! 'There's a special legend about me. Shall I tell you?'

'Why, yes, if you'd like to.'

'Apparently the girl I was destined to marry was beautiful, intelligent and kind, but had a bad hump on her back. The angels were very worried about this, for they knew that, however beautiful a girl might be, a hump would detract from her charms in worldly eyes. You see, we're far more particular on earth than the angels are in heaven. We mortals pick and choose and only judge people by outward appearances.

'Well, I overheard the angels discussing this girl. They were afraid that her hump would make her morose, self-conscious and unhappy, and they didn't know what they could do about it. I began to feel sorry for her, too, so I went up to the angels and offered to have the hump laid upon my shoulders instead. They were very surprised at my suggestion, but were so relieved to think that this lovely girl could be spared from such an affliction that they agreed at once. And some years after I was born a hump began to grow on my shoulders.

'I'm very glad it did,' went on Moses gently. 'It didn't bother me much when I was younger, and now that I have met you I am thankful the angels allowed me to have the hump and didn't insist that it belonged to you. Although, to me, you would always be lovely – hump or no hump!'

As Moses ended his story he saw tears streaming down Fromet's face. Then, to his utmost relief, she flung down her needlework and came over to him. He held out his arms, and drew her close.

Fromet rested her cheek against his. 'Thank you very much,' she said, half laughing, half crying. 'I should have hated to have a hump!'

'Then it's lucky I walked by while the angels were discussing you! Has my story altered things at all? Do you think now you could live with me and be my

89

wife? I should always love you, and I would honour you and cherish you and look after you every day of my life.'

Moses' look of anguish and appeal melted Fromet's heart. A tranquil, happy expression came over her face as she said softly, 'Yes, I will be your wife. I want to be now . . . I know my father would like me to be . . . and if the angels expect it too – well, then, there's nothing more to say. . . .'

'Except perhaps, that one day you will come to love me. The angels would be very disappointed if you didn't.'

'All right,' laughed Fromet. 'I will – I think I do a little already.'

Moses kissed her gently, his heart leaping with joy. Fromet, sweet and lovely Fromet, was to be his bride. He had never before known such happiness. 'Shall we tell your parents?' he suggested, coming down to earth, though he still stared dreamily into her eyes. 'They're expecting at any moment to see a sad suitor walking down the stairs.'

There was pandemonium in the Gugenheim household when Fromet broke the news. They all embraced each other, the dogs barked excitedly, and Fromet's two budgerigars chattered loudly.

It was some time before things quietened down and they talked again in normal tones. Moses said at once that he would delay his return to Berlin, and during the days that followed all the plans were made. Moses and Fromet were to have a year's engagement, and after their marriage – in June, 1762 – they would settle in Berlin.

There was much to discuss, and Moses and Herr Gugenheim spent several mornings together. On one occasion Herr Gugenheim voiced his only fear about the future. 'I can see, Moses, that you must remain in Berlin, but you are not even a Protected Jew. I know you are honoured for your learning and your writings, but nevertheless you are in a very perilous position as far as your status in the city is concerned.'

Moses leaned forward and spoke intently. 'I do most sincerely hope – and believe – that this situation will soon be altered. Before I left for Hamburg I asked a friend, the Marquis d'Argens, to present a petition on my behalf seeking his Majesty's protection. I have no great fortune – which would, of course, influence the King's decision! – but I am hoping that my work in the sciences will make up for my lack of money. As soon as I return to Berlin I will find out what decision has been taken.'

Moses kept his word. He understood Herr Gugenheim's concern, which was, in fact, only less than his own. A few days later he left Hamburg, with Fromet's kisses and loving words to make the parting less painful. The moment he arrived in Berlin he sought a meeting with the Marquis d'Argens.

They met the following morning at the coffee-house. Moses was sitting at his usual corner table half-an-hour before the appointed time, and he sighed with relief when the elegantly dressed Marquis at last came sauntering through the door. Moses rose from the bench as his friend walked over to him. He was so anxious about the outcome of the petition that he could not bring himself to speak.

The Marquis stood facing him, and then regretfully shook his head. 'I'm sorry, Moses, but I have bad news for you. I presented your petition, but the King ignored it. While you were in Hamburg I mentioned it to him several times, but he immediately began to talk of other things. I am afraid he will not even discuss your petition, let alone grant it!'

And so, despite the fact that Moses had lived in Berlin for eighteen years, and had worked hard in the cause of literature, learning, philosophy and the sciences, he could remain in the city only on sufferance. His position was on a par with the stray dogs and cats that stalked the streets of the ghetto.

CHAPTER EIGHT

Literary Honours

MOSES and Fromet spent their honeymoon in a small country inn which belonged to a friend of Herr Gugenheim's. The sun shone, the countryside was beautiful, and they both felt they hadn't a care in the world.

In a letter which Moses sent to Thomas Abt, Professor of Philosophy at Frankfort University, he said, 'For some weeks past, I have neither spoken nor written to a friend, I have neither thought nor read nor written anything. I have only been dallying, feasting, observing sacred ceremonies. . . . A blue-eyed girl whom I now call my wife has dissolved the chilly heart of your friend into feelings and has entangled his mind in a thousand distractions from which it now seeks to disentangle itself gradually. . . .'

As the holiday drew to an end Moses and Fromet found themselves looking forward to starting life in their new home in Berlin. With the small dowry that Herr Gugenheim had given to them they had

93

bought a modest house on the outskirts of the city. Moses had been able to furnish it, thanks to Herr Bernhard's generosity, for when his employer had heard of his engagement he had improved his status in the firm and had made him a manager in the factory.

Moses had described the house and garden to Fromet, who was eager to know every detail. 'You'll be able to change things round,' said Moses on the journey home. 'I'm not much good at arranging ornaments and. . . .'

'I shall love using the beautiful china tea-service,' said Fromet, thinking excitedly of their wedding presents. 'I do like china.'

'Oh . . . do you?' said Moses awkwardly, and then changed the subject. Fromet noticed and wondered but said nothing. After a moment she forgot about it.

But she remembered again the moment they stepped inside the front door. Fromet had exclaimed with delight as the carriage had set them down outside a white-painted cottage situated in a small garden. She had hurried up the path, and could hardly wait for Moses to open the door. Hand in hand, they had stepped over the threshhold — and it was then that Fromet gave a wild shriek of terror.

'LOOK! LOOK THERE! WHATEVER ARE THEY?'

Moses bit his lip and looked unhappy. 'Don't be frightened, Fromet. They're not real. I didn't tell

94

you about them before because I was afraid it might spoil our honeymoon. But when I went along to the Royal Porcelain Factory to buy the required amount of china, I was obliged to take twenty-two of these hideous ornamental apes.'

'*Ornamental!*' breathed Fromet, and sank weakly into a chair. Ruefully she and Moses looked at each other. Fromet knew that when a Jew married he was ordered by law to buy a certain quantity of china from the royal factories. But she had never dreamt that the factory would make – let alone force her husband to take – such useless and grotesque ornaments. Why, the apes were almost life-size!

'I'm *really* sorry, Fromet. I had no choice at all. I don't know what we can do with them.'

'Break them!' suggested Fromet hopefully.

'They're almost too solid for that, but perhaps we'll get used to them in time.'

'I can't imagine anything worse than apes!' said Fromet, still despondent.

Moses thought for a moment, then, with a twinkle in his eye, murmured, 'Well, they might have made me take dinosaurs!'

Fromet hadn't intended her remark to be taken literally, and she frowned. But then she caught sight of her husband's worried gaze, and almost immediately her annoyance vanished. After all, it wasn't Moses' fault, and he would have to live in the same house with them, too! 'Let's look round the house and try and forget the apes.'

Relieved at her change of mood, Moses quickly agreed, though he was afraid it would be difficult to forget the apes as they were in every room.

Hand in hand they explored the house. First they went into the narrow kitchen and Fromet exclaimed with delight as they looked out of the window on to the garden, which had a well in the centre of a neat square lawn. Then they walked back into the hall and entered the main downstairs room. This contained some chairs with padded seats, two ornamental apes, a low glass cabinet, and, on either side of the fireplace, plain wooden bookcases. Looking a little out of place, yet giving an air of magnificence to the low-ceilinged room, were some fine gold silk curtains – a gift from Herr Bernhard.

Leading out of this living-room was a much smaller room which had a window. Fromet agreed with Moses that this would be an ideal place for him to study and work undisturbed. There was also a small dining-room across the hall.

There were three tiny bedrooms upstairs: one was furnished for themselves, the others contained most of their wedding presents – as well as the inevitable apes!

Although the house was small and unpretentious, neither Moses nor Fromet wished for anything more. They were both happy and because of this their home was a true haven.

Moses got up early and spent each day at the silk factory, and all the while he longed for the evenings when he could be home again with his bride. In this frame of mind it would have been easy for Moses to spend all his free time just looking at and talking to Fromet, but as the weeks passed he felt he must start writing again. Lessing was still living away from Berlin, and Moses found that without his friend's enthusiasm and encouragement he no longer had the same interest in literary criticism. Instead, his thoughts turned to his old love, philosophy.

Then, in 1763, the Berlin Royal Academy of Sciences made an announcement about its annual competition, and this provided a real incentive for Moses to return to work. The Academy offered a prize of fifty ducats and a medal for an essay on a philosophical subject that particularly intrigued Moses and he set to work once more.

Soon after he had sent in his essay he discovered that his friend, Thomas Abt, and Immanuel Kant, the renowned philosopher and lecturer at the University of Königsberg, were among the competitors. Both these brilliant men belonged to a learned guild, and had had the advantages of a good, all-round education – while it was not so many years ago that Moses did not even know the German alphabet!

Moses wondered whether to withdraw his essay, but then decided against this course. The only thing for him to do, he told himself, was to forget he had ever entered the competition.

On June 4th, 1763, the result of the Academy's competition was announced. Moses could scarcely believe his eyes when he read in a newspaper that he was the winner! He was to be awarded the prize . . . he, and not the brilliant Immanuel Kant nor the learned Thomas Abt!

Excitement followed excitement, and in October of the same year Moses received the distinction of being made a Protected Jew. Rumour had it that the Marquis d'Argens at last persuaded King Frederick to grant Moses' petition by saying: 'A bad Catholic philosopher begs a bad Protestant philosopher to grant the privilege to a bad Jewish philosopher. There is too much philosophy in all this for justice not to be on the side of the request.'

Now, for the first time since he had lived in Berlin, Moses felt he had been accepted by the community. Being a Jew was no longer a drawback – he had fought many battles against religious prejudices, but now, it seemed, the victory was his.

Moses tried not to be too conceited about his success, but he was not really surprised when Immanuel Kant asked him to lecture at the University of Königsberg. After all, he had won the Berlin Academy's prize – it was only natural that the students should want to hear him speak on philosophy.

When he reached the University on the morning that he was due to lecture, Kant met him in the hall and said he would introduce him to the students. Moses had prepared his lecture well, and felt more confident than ever before. Deep in discussion, the two men walked down the long corridor towards the lecture hall. Kant pushed open the door, and Moses followed him inside.

About a hundred students were sitting on benches facing the platform; many others were leaning against the walls or standing in groups by the windows. Moses glanced round the large lecture room, feeling very flattered at the high attendance, and marched forward down the aisle.

Moses smiled about him, but was met with stony glares. Then there came a strange sound from the back of the room. Moses was puzzled for a moment, but the sound came again . . . and then again. Then the truth dawned upon him. The students were hissing!

Moses felt the colour drain from his face. He stopped suddenly, wishing the floor would open up and swallow him. He thought of turning round and fleeing, but found he couldn't even move!

'Jew, go home!'

'We don't want Jews in here!'

The hissing grew louder, the taunts were shouted from everywhere. Moses was astounded. Had he been invited to the University merely to be insulted? It was obvious that none of the students wanted to hear him speak.

Then, in a few strides, Kant was beside him. He linked arms with Moses, and led him on.

Gradually the hissing died away. By the time the two men reached the platform there was silence in the hall. Moses bowed his head in misery. Five minutes ago he had been looking forward to it all – but now he didn't want to give his lecture, he didn't want to face the students. Then he felt Kant's hand upon his shoulder, and gently but firmly he found himself being pushed forward.

Moses forced himself to raise his head, and stared at the unfriendly sea of faces before him – but still he could not speak.

Then, from the back of the hall, came a single handclap. Then there came another. There was a low buzz of conversation among the students, and gradually one after another decided to follow suit. In a few minutes the hall was resounding with applause. At last Moses' voice returned to him. He acknowledged the new situation with a smile, and, as the clapping died away, he began his lecture.

By this time the students were regretting the hostile reception which they had given to a visiting speaker. They decided to make amends by listening with the greatest attention.

Though stammering more than usual, Moses managed to get through his lecture. When he had finished he invited questions, and was relieved that many were politely asked of him. Then one of the senior students rose to his feet and thanked Moses for coming along. His speech was short, but there was no doubt of its sincerity.

Even so, Moses breathed a sigh of relief when he finally said good-bye to Immanuel Kant, and clambered aboard the coach which would take him away from the University grounds.

He was glad to reach home that night, and to see Fromet happily settling their baby daughter, Dorothea, to sleep. As soon as he entered the room, however, Fromet leapt to her feet and rushed over to him. With her voice full of excitement she told Moses that Herr Bernhard had called that afternoon. 'I said you would soon be home, but he was too busy to wait. He wants to see you first thing to-morrow morning at the factory because he's going to make you a partner in the firm!'

Moses could hardly believe this to be true. Fromet often muddled the messages, and he was sure she must have done so this time. But next morning Herr Bernhard told him the news himself, and Moses spent the rest of the day walking on air. To be a partner in Herr Bernhard's silk factory would put an end to all his financial worries. It would mean his livelihood was secure, and so was the future of his wife and daughter. And, in his spare time, he would still be able to carry on with his own reading and writing!

His own studying was very important to him at the moment, for he had just started writing a book called *Phaedon, or The Immortality of the Soul.* Many of his friends – Christians as well as Jewish – often came to his house in the evenings to talk about religion, and sometimes they said they didn't really believe that God existed or that the soul and the body were the work of God. Moses tried hard to convince them

101

they were wrong, but he was not always successful. In *Phaedon* he explained all the reasons why he considered the soul to be immortal.

Phaedon was published in 1767, and was an immediate and outstanding success. It was translated into many European languages and also into Hebrew. Soon afterwards Moses heard that the Berlin Academy of Sciences had included his name on their list of prospective members – and the list had already gone forward to King Frederick for his approval. For some time Moses had secretly longed to become a member of the Academy, and he was very excited to think that his dream was about to come true.

But disappointment followed. A few days later Moses heard that King Frederick had struck his name off the list of proposed Academy members. The Prussian ruler declared that he wanted the Empress Catherine of Russia admitted into that learned body, and he did not want to insult her by allowing a Jew to be a fellow-member!

CHAPTER NINE

A Challenge

ONE evening the usual crowd gathered at Moses'
house—which was now an accepted meeting-
place for intellectuals. Someone had brought a friend
along, and he was warmly welcomed by Moses and
Fromet. His name was Johann Lavater, and he told
Moses he was a pastor in Switzerland.

At ten o'clock Fromet handed round nuts, raisins,
sweetmeats and coffee. She always counted out the
number of nuts and raisins which could be eaten by
the family, so that there were enough left for their
guests. Sometimes she wished Moses could let her
have more money for housekeeping: it wasn't easy
to feed and clothe themselves, let alone provide re-
freshments for all their visitors. Whenever she
grumbled about it, though, Moses would tell her
that people only came to the house to talk, they
didn't want anything to eat. But he didn't really
mean it – and Fromet knew it!

That day, in 1763, Johann Lavater licked his lips

103

in appreciation as he swallowed the last morsel of one of Fromet's biscuits. 'I've never had such an interesting discussion, nor tasted such delicious biscuits,' he murmured as he took another from the silver tray. 'I shall never forget this evening!'

Nor, as it turned out, did Moses and Fromet, though at the time it had seemed like so many others. Everyone had talked heatedly about Judaism and Christianity, while Moses sat back in his armchair and listened. He preferred to hear all the different points of view, and then give his own when everyone was exhausted by arguing.

At one point Lavater suddenly turned to Moses and said, 'I wish you'd tell us exactly what you think of Jesus.'

Moses hated getting involved in this sort of conversation and he tried hard to change the subject, but Lavater insisted on an answer. When he saw he could not get out of it, Moses made everyone promise never to make any *public* use of what he was about to say in *private* conversation. Then he said that he thought Jesus only wished to lead a good and holy life. 'I would have had some respect for him,' Moses added, 'if he hadn't accepted the homage which is due only to God Almighty.'

All his guests looked at him in amazement. They never expected a Jew to regard the founder of Christianity in such an unbiased way. Someone said that they appreciated Moses' fair-mindedness, and, on behalf of them all, promised again that no one would repeat anything he had said that evening.

Six years later, in the summer of 1769, Moses remembered that discussion as vividly as if it had been the previous day. He wasn't well at the time, and the doctor had advised him to stay in bed. He was a difficult patient, for, after the first morning, he was utterly bored.

Fromet had her hands full already with Dorothea, who was now six, and with their two other daughters, Recha and Henriette. Every time she brought the meals upstairs to the bedroom, she felt even more harassed, for Moses would look at her in a long-suffering way and ask for a different book to read.

'You'll never get well if you won't rest,' she said irritably, when Moses complained that he had finished the book she had brought him earlier that morning. 'The doctor said you've been working much too hard. I don't know why you won't do what he tells you!'

'I can't just lie here and do nothing. I hate wasting time. Listen, there's someone coming up the path. I wonder who it is!'

Fromet walked over to the window and peered outside. 'Oh, it's one of the students from the university. He's carrying something. . . .'

'Perhaps it's something new for me to read. Do hurry down, Fromet, and see what he's got!'

Fromet turned away, and murmuring, 'Haven't I got enough to do without running up and down the stairs all day?' disappeared from the room.

D•

A few minutes later she was back, slightly ashamed of being irritable. Moses sat up excitedly as she came through the door, and held out his hand for the parcel Fromet was carrying. 'Now you look happy again,' said Fromet, smiling at the eager way her husband was unwrapping the paper. 'I'd better get on with my work while I can.'

Fromet was half-way down the stairs when she heard a sudden cry. Horrified, she rushed back into the bedroom. 'What's happened?'

'Look! Look at this!' Moses held out a slim volume, and pointed to a long paragraph.

Fromet felt exasperation welling up inside her. 'I'm much too busy to read your books. I thought something was wrong.'

'You were right!' Moses stared at the page again, and sank back exhausted on his pillow. 'Don't look so cross,' he murmured, making an effort to smile. 'I've just had a dreadful shock. Do you remember Johann Lavater?'

Fromet thought for a second. 'Yes . . . yes, of course. He was the man who ate most of my biscuits. Why?'

'Lavater has translated a book by Charles Bonnet – the famous naturalist. In this work Bonnet has tried to prove the truth of Christianity, and Lavater has dedicated his translation to me. He demands that I either publicly refute what Bonnet has said, or, if I can't do that, then I should renounce Judaism and become a Christian.'

Fromet was obviously puzzled, so Moses went on to explain. 'We were talking about religion the evening Lavater was here. After everyone had promised not to repeat anything I said, I gave my considered opinion of the founder of Christianity. Lavater has made use of my remarks to try to prove that I am not really convinced of the truth of Judaism.'

'Why must you reply to him?' demanded Fromet.

'If I don't, it will look as though I can't disprove Bonnet's arguments. But if I do reply, I shall have publicly to attack Christianity – the accepted religion of Prussia. However much King Frederick may sneer at the State religion, he won't approve – and quite rightly – of a Jew attacking it.'

Moses spent the rest of the day worrying over his predicament. He felt he must consider the matter very carefully, and not come to any hasty decision. But in his heart he knew that there was only one course open to him: whatever risks might be involved and however much he might dislike the task, he must publicly give his reply.

Once he had made up his mind Moses allowed himself no peace. All his efforts went to composing an answer to Lavater. In vain did Fromet and his doctor appeal to him to rest and relax; for Moses, this would have been impossible.

Within a short time every member of the learned circle knew about Lavater's challenge, and many of Moses' friends came to visit him at home. They told him that several people were saying laughingly that he was about to shave off his beard and become a Christian. Lavater's followers, meanwhile, were looking forward to the day when Moses would renounce Judaism and embrace Christianity. They then expected that thousands of other Jews would follow his example.

These reports made Moses even more angry, and he worked both day and night until he was satisfied with his reply.

At the beginning of 1770 a long letter from Moses to Lavater appeared before the public. First of all, Moses reproved him for making use of a confidential conversation which they had had many years ago. He then went on to say that he was firmly opposed to Christianity for the reason he had already given to Lavater – and that was because its founder had identified himself with God.

Moses admitted that he was aware of 'certain human additions and base alloy in Judaism which, alas! but too much tarnish its pristine lustre'. But, he went on, no religion is free from similar corruptions, and of the essentials of *his* religion he was as firmly convinced as Herr Lavater or Herr Bonnet could ever be of theirs!

He then gave the reasons why he did not wish to be involved in religious controversy, and said he hoped Lavater would excuse him from the irksome task of refuting Herr Bonnet's work.

To Moses' great relief his letter had the desired

effect. Lavater withdrew his challenge and publicly apologised for having put him in such an embarrassing position.

But that was not the end of the matter. Some time afterwards, when Moses was up and about again, one of the most Orthodox members of the synagogue called to see him. Moses was sitting at his desk when Fromet showed the visitor into the study. He rose to his feet, and greeted him with a smile.

His gesture was met with a dignified and stony stare. 'Herr Mendelssohn,' said the elderly man, who was dressed in flowing black robes. 'I had intended to ask you to speak to us in our synagogue hall. . . .'

There was a pause, and Moses, greatly puzzled, felt he was expected to say something. 'Well, I should be honoured to do so. What is the subject to be discussed?'

'Nothing that can concern you!' came the stern and astonishing reply. 'It is no longer the wish of the Elders of the congregation that you should address us. They have asked me to call to express our horror and disgust at your recent letter to Herr Lavater. We can no longer respect a man who feels that "human additions and base alloy tarnish the pristine lustre of Judaism".'

Moses was aghast. 'But that was only one of the things that I said. . . .'

'That was more than enough!' With that, the man stalked from the room and made his way out of the house. Moses was too surprised to accompany him.

He simply sank back into his chair with a gesture of bewilderment.

'That settles it! Never again shall I become involved in religious controversy,' he vowed, as he picked up his pen and returned to his work. 'Religion is a matter of individual conscience, and not of public argument!'

But this was a vow that Moses was not to keep.

CHAPTER TEN

Disaster Upon Disaster!

MOSES felt that time was passing all too quickly. He and Fromet had been married now for twelve years; they had three daughters and a four-year-old son, Joseph. They often talked about moving to a larger house in Berlin, for much as they loved their present home it was too small to hold their family, their parents (who occasionally managed to visit them in Berlin) and their servant-girl.

Moses' house was still the accepted place for his friends and colleagues to congregate. He loved to see the living-room filled with people, and to listen to them talking about every subject under the sun. He really preferred to listen, rather than to join in, but now and again he would add a few words on matters about which he felt strongly. When discussions grew very heated, his friends would sometimes turn to Moses – almost as though he were the umpire.

One Friday, in the late afternoon, a few of them were sitting round Moses' fireside pleasantly passing

111

the time by talking. Someone happened to mention a now almost forgotten subject, Johann Lavater's translation of Bonnet's book, and the others began talking about the merits of the work. A keen young Christian professor declared his whole-hearted praise for the translation, another violently disagreed with him. Within minutes each was trying to make his own voice heard above the others.

Then someone noticed that Moses had disappeared from the room, and the clamour of conversation died away.

'How tactless of us to talk about Bonnet!'

'Perhaps we've offended him so much that he won't come back.'

'Let's find him, and apologise.'

Everyone looked very guilty, for they felt they had abused Moses' hospitality by talking about something which they knew he did not want to discuss. A couple of them agreed to seek out Moses and tell him how sorry they all were.

They thought they might find him with Fromet in the kitchen, but although there was a delicious smell from the stew which was cooking slowly in the large cauldron suspended above the fire, the room itself was empty. Then they wondered if he had retired to his study, but there too they were disappointed.

The only place left downstairs was the dining-room, so they crossed the hall and opened another door. They peered inside, gasped, and then stood there fascinated by the sight that met their eyes.

Fromet was lighting the Sabbath candles, and, as she did so, was pronouncing the ancient blessing. Moses was standing by her side, the prayer-book open before him. As Fromet finished speaking, they smiled at each other.

Quietly, without their noticing it, the dining-room door was closed. Their guests crept back into the study and told the others what they had seen. Moses had always commanded a certain amount of admiration from his friends, and that evening the admiration increased. For then they realised in a way they had never done before that Moses not only discussed Judaism, but conscientiously and sincerely observed its customs.

Moses and Fromet did indeed try to keep the spirit of Judaism alive in their home, and Moses would patiently explain their religion to the children. For a few years the two eldest – Dorothea and Recha – were particularly interested, and loved to hear their father chanting the traditional hymns. Then suddenly, one day, they stopped paying attention. Moses could not understand why they no longer wanted to hear Bible stories, or to practise writing the letters of the Hebrew alphabet – which had once fascinated them so much. But when he asked them the reason they just shrugged their shoulders and stared blankly at him.

This went on for some time, with Moses getting angrier as their interest in their lessons decreased. He had successfully instructed Herr Bernhard's children, and he was determined that his own should be equally well informed. One morning he became really cross when Dorothea and Recha refused to pay attention, and he told them he would not let them go to their friend's Barmitzvah party which had been arranged for that afternoon. At first they protested noisily, but when they saw their father was determined they became sulky and behaved as though they were even more bored with their lessons than before.

Fromet was busy mending the children's clothes, so after lunch Moses agreed to take Dorothea, Recha, Henriette and Joseph for a walk. He was secretly regretting that he had decided on that particular punishment for Dorothea and Recha, for if he had allowed them to go to the party he could have got on with his own writing – which he was most anxious to do. But he felt he could not go back on his word, so, with an ill grace, he shepherded the children down the street and then across the fields towards the woods.

The walk proved a disaster. The children returned home in tears, and Dorothea had a cut across her forehead. Moses, however, though pale with anger, felt as though a load had been lifted from his mind – he knew now why his children had lost their interest in religion, and it was not through any fault of his own.

After they had left the busy streets a group of young boys had followed them. At first Moses took no notice, even when they had started jeering. He could not quite hear what they were saying, but then he rounded on them angrily and told them to go away. At that point trouble really started.

The leader of the group, a tall, lanky boy, shouted insolently: 'You've no right to be in Berlin! You're only Jews!'

Someone pointed to little Joseph, and yelled, 'Jew-boy! Jew-boy!'

There was some laughter from the other young ruffians, who were by this time jumping around them in a circle. Suddenly Dorothea screamed. Moses spun round, and saw blood streaming from her forehead.

'He hurt me! That boy threw a stone at me!' Dorothea sobbed, and pointed to a ginger-headed boy with a snub nose, who was grinning widely.

'Jews! Jews! Who cares about Jews!' The boys began chanting together, but then they hesitated as Moses rushed at them. Easily evading him – he was, after all, a small man and a hunchback into the bargain – the boys slipped through his grasp and ran away across the fields.

Henriette and Recha were by this time screaming even more loudly than Dorothea, and Moses did not know whom to comfort first. He wiped the blood from Dorothea's forehead, and felt a strange stab of anguish as Joseph asked, 'Father, is it wicked to be a Jew?'

'Why don't they like us? What have we done wrong?' demanded Henriette through her sobs. 'I

115

wish we weren't Jewish!' she added in a pathetic tone, which wrung her father's heart.

On the way home he gathered that this had happened before, though not with such disastrous results. Dorothea and Henriette told him that hooligans often shouted at them in the streets when they were taken out by the servant-girl. 'We don't like being Jewish,' said Dorothea, as they walked up the path towards their house. 'That's why we don't want to learn about religion!' she ended up, deciding on the spur of the moment that there was no point in keeping this a secret any longer.

What could he say? His children were too young to understand that prejudices take long to die. For generations Jews had been despised. Now the more enlightened Germans were beginning to learn to tolerate them, but this was a heart-breakingly slow process. Moses was convinced that, in time, Germans would come to accept Jews as their equals – but he found it hard to convince his children that this would be the case.

Moses suddenly felt overwhelmed with problems. He was worried about the effect such incidents would have on his children, but, even more than that, he was worried at the intolerance and harshness with which Jews were treated. He was concerned, too, about a book which his friend Lessing had planned to have published. This book was written by Professor Samuel Reimarus, who was against religion of every sort – Christian as well as Jewish. There was so much cynicism and disbelief about religion, and Moses could not understand why Lessing should deliberately make things worse by publishing such a work.

On top of all this, Herr Bernhard had been in bad health for some time, and Moses was kept even busier at the factory. Then, when he came home and had had a meal, he would spend several hours at his books; however busy he was at the factory, he still read and wrote about religious and philosophical subjects. Moses knew he was overworking, but he could not bring himself to take things more easily.

One Friday, after a particularly tiring week, he returned home in the late afternoon utterly exhausted. He rested for an hour on his bed, and, though he slept fitfully, he felt just as tired when he came downstairs to join his family for the Sabbath evening meal.

Dorothea, Recha and Henriette stayed up for dinner on Friday nights, and they looked forward eagerly to the treat. On this evening they were all wearing crimson velvet dresses with white lace collars and cuffs. Their hair had been carefully combed, and when they appeared at the table, looking so clean and quiet, it was hard to believe they had been making such a noise a little while earlier.

Fromet kept her finest white damask tablecloth for the Sabbath evening meal, and her silver candlesticks and tableware glistened from hard polishing. A large china dish filled with fruit provided the centre-piece,

117

and small glass finger-bowls were placed at intervals round the table.

Through the tiredness that half-blinded him, Moses watched Fromet lighting the candles, and felt strangely moved.

He opened the prayer-book and raised the silver goblet as he pronounced the ancient benediction: 'Blessed art thou, O Lord our God, King of the Universe, who createst the fruit of the vine.' His voice trembled slightly, and Fromet was horrified to see the white, drawn expression on his face. She knew he was worn out with work and worry, so she tried to keep the children quiet during the meal that followed.

Moses found it too great an effort to eat the food which Fromet placed before him. He scarcely touched the *lockshen* soup, and only ate a few mouthfuls of the deliciously tender chicken which had been roasted over the blazing charcoal fire in the kitchen. He sat patiently as Fromet and the children helped themselves to fruit and nuts and raisins, but he could not manage anything himself.

When the meal was over, Moses recited grace, and then they sang their favourite Friday night table-song. Dorothea and Recha loudly and enthusiastically led the singing:

Thou beautiful Sabbath, thou sanctified day,
That chasest our cares and our sorrows away;
O come with good fortune, with joy and with peace,
To honour thee, Sabbath, thou day of sweet rest!

DISASTER UPON DISASTER!

In honour of thee are the tables decked white,
From the clear candelabra shine many a light;
All men in the finest of garments are dress'd,
As far as his purse, each hath got him the best.

New heavenly powers are given to each,
Of everyday matters now hush'd is all speech;
At rest are all hands that have toil'd with much pain,
Now peace and tranquillity everywhere reign.

Not the choicest of wines at a banqueting board,
Can ever such exquisite pleasure afford;
As the Friday-night meal when prepared with due zest,
To honour thee, Sabbath, thou day of sweet rest![1]

Fromet leaned back in her chair and smiled at her husband. She would make him rest during the week-end, she would not let him exert himself in any way at all.

'Let's sing some more,' said Recha, who was reluctant to leave the table for she knew she and her sisters would be sent to bed immediately afterwards.

But Moses had already risen from his chair. He stood at the head of the table, his eyes closed. He felt himself swaying, and he put a hand on the table to steady himself.

Fromet stared at him aghast. 'Moses, Moses!' she cried. 'Are you all right?' She jumped up from her chair to hurry round to him.

[1]The quotation from the song comes from Israel Abrahams' *Jewish Life in the Middle Ages*, published by Macmillan & Co. Ltd.

'Yes . . . I'm only a little tired,' murmured Moses, and tried to smile.

He took one step, and staggered. Horror-stricken, his family watched as he collapsed in a crumpled heap on the floor.

CHAPTER ELEVEN

Fighting Intolerance

IN a second, Fromet was kneeling beside her husband. 'Moses,' she whispered, then almost swooned with relief when she realised he was still breathing. She sent Dorothea hurrrying to the kitchen with instructions to their servant-girl to rush to the doctor. Recha followed fast on her sister's heels, and returned a few moments later with some water, which Fromet threw over Moses' face to help him regain consciousness.

Within ten minutes the doctor arrived with his assistant. Moses was carried up the stairs to bed, and shortly afterwards he opened his eyes and tried to speak. The doctor examined him, and soon gave his verdict. Moses had worked himself into a state of exhaustion, and would need six weeks of complete rest to recover. 'On no account must your husband read, write or strain himself in any way, Frau Mendelssohn,' warned the doctor. 'That is the only way he can recover from this breakdown!'

After the doctor had gone Fromet told the children that they would have to keep very quiet and behave especially well. They all assured her that they would; and, as it was now long past their bed-time, they meekly trooped upstairs.

For quite a long time they kept their promise. Dorothea and Recha helped their mother look after Henriette and Joseph, so that she could spend most of the day seeing to Moses' needs. Gradually he began to make progress, and then Fromet really had her hands full. For Moses, never an easy patient, hated being in bed, and did everything he could to persuade Fromet to bring him some books from the study. She steadfastly refused, even though he grew irritable and depressed in turn.

The strain of looking after such a difficult invalid began to tell, and, during one of his visits, the doctor noticed how tired and pale Fromet had become.

'This won't do at all,' he said, glancing at her. 'You'll be ill, too, if you carry on like this. Herr Mendelssohn, you must make your wife take a walk every day: she must have fresh air if she's to keep well enough to look after you!'

Moses felt very contrite. He had been so busy feeling sorry for himself that he had never noticed the pallor on Fromet's face. 'Of course she must have a walk each day,' he said at once. 'Anyway, I'm feeling so well that I could get up and look after myself now. Surely it wouldn't do me any harm if I read occasionally, doctor?'

The doctor shook his head. 'You must wait till you're better,' he insisted. 'I shall call again in a few days, and perhaps then you'll be able to get out of bed for a few minutes.'

This cheered Moses considerably. At least it would be progress – even if it were only a few minutes! And he faithfully kept his word to the doctor, and persuaded Fromet to take a stroll in the garden or along the streets every single afternoon.

While she was out, Dorothea was in charge. Although she was only eleven, she was mature for her years and behaved more like a girl of fourteen. She thoroughly enjoyed waiting on her father, and giving orders to the servant, who, though not very bright, was always willing to do as she was told. If visitors – other than her parents' friends – called at the house, Dorothea hurried to the front door and, as instructed by her mother, sent them away. For no one was allowed to worry Moses on any matter whatsoever.

One afternoon, while Fromet was out, Dorothea and Recha were sitting in the garden, reading in the shade of an old linden tree. They looked up as they heard footsteps, and saw a tall, dark-haired man in his early twenties making his way towards the house. Dorothea walked over to him, intending to send him away, but, as she reached him, she stopped and stared. He was so good-looking and had such a nice smile that she hesitated.

'May I speak to Herr Mendelssohn, please?'

'No, I'm afraid you can't,' replied Dorothea. 'My

father's been very ill, and the doctor has forbade him visitors.'

'But I'll only stay a few minutes, and it's terribly important. Won't you *please* let me have just a word with him?' He looked imploringly at Dorothea, who felt it would almost be cruel to resist a request from such a charming person. Anyway, her father was now much better and was always complaining he was bored. Perhaps it would cheer him up to see this man.

'Well, you'll have to be quick about it. Mother will be back in half an hour and she'll be very angry if she finds you here.'

'Let's hurry, then,' said the young man, whose name, he told her as they walked swiftly towards the house, was David.

Dorothea was almost sorry when they reached the top of the stairs and David disappeared into her father's bedroom. She hung around on the landing, waiting for him to come out, and keeping a look-out for her mother.

Moses was astonished to see a strange figure appearing at his bedside, but he was delighted just the same. He was longing to talk to people again.

David wasted no time in telling him why he had come. 'I represent the Jewish communities in Endingen and Lengnau in Switzerland, and we are all in desperate trouble. As you know, we are allowed to settle only in these villages, and we have always lived and worked quietly and have done our best never to offend the authorities. But they have now issued a decree forbidding us to marry, and we do not know what to do. We have appealed against this cruel restriction, but they refuse to listen to us. We know you have influence among many Christians in high and influential positions, and we beg you to intercede for us.'

Before Moses had time to answer, the door burst open and a worried-looking Fromet appeared on the scene. 'I shall never leave the children in charge again,' she declared in agitated tones, and then, turning to David, begged him to leave her husband in peace. To her surprise he agreed, though before turning to the door he murmured in a low voice to Moses, 'Can you help us? Will you help us? Otherwise, how can we survive?'

'I'll do my best,' replied Moses in a determined voice, and then lay back on his pillow, pretending to look as though the effort of talking to the stranger had not in the least exhausted him. But Fromet knew otherwise, and spent the next fifteen minutes trying to persuade him to forget all about David's problems.

'How can I forget about Jews in lands not far away who are being persecuted?' demanded Moses. 'If I can help them, surely you would have me do it?'

Fromet just stared at Moses helplessly. She knew her husband's mind was made up, and there was nothing she could do to change it. All she could say was, 'Moses, don't make yourself ill again . . . please.'

Moses scarcely heard her. He was busy thinking what he should do. 'I shall write to Lavater. . . .'

125

'I wouldn't have thought you would want to get in touch with that man again. Think how badly he behaved to you before.'

'Well, he did apologise,' grinned Moses. Then he closed his eyes and put his hand to his forehead, as he planned what he should say.

That same day the letter was completed. Moses placed the facts clearly before Lavater, and said that he knew only what his visitor had told him. He appealed to the Swiss pastor to use his influence and arrange for this unjust edict to be withdrawn.

A short time later Moses learned that Lavater had acted promptly on receiving his letter and had managed to persuade the Swiss authorities to cancel their decree. As a result, many Jewish hearts went out in gratitude to Moses, and people began to feel there existed among them a champion of their race, a man to whom they could turn when religious persecution came their way.

It was therefore natural that Moses should hear of injustices against his co-religionists whenever and wherever they were perpetrated. If he could, Moses would intercede and his reputation for wisdom was now sufficiently great to make despotic rulers hesitate to carry out harsh edicts in face of protests from the Jewish philosopher.

On one occasion – in 1777 – hundreds of poverty-stricken Jews were ordered to leave the city of Dresden because they could not afford to pay their personal tax on the stipulated day. Moses wrote indignantly on their behalf to Privy Councillor Freiherr von Ferber of the Prince Elector's Court, whom he had met the previous year. Von Ferber wielded great influence in Saxony, and he was taken aback by the vehemence of Moses' protest.

He at once called his fellow-councillors together, and solemnly read aloud Moses' letter. There was a silence – almost of shame – in the council chamber when he came to the end, and not a voice was raised in disagreement when von Ferber announced that the decree against the Jews was to be rescinded.

When Moses heard that his letter had achieved its object, an extraordinary feeling – not of pride, but of humility – came over him. Perhaps people were at last beginning to hearken to the ancient Biblical command: 'Thou shalt love thy neighbour as thyself.' And, in a small way, perhaps he had helped.

Were thoughts of justice, were feelings of love and charity, at last beginning to stir in the minds of men, he wondered? As harsh edicts were repealed, as knowledge and understanding began slowly to take the place of bigotry and age-long prejudice, Moses felt there was hope for humanity.

But despite some few encouraging signs, discord and disunity among religious thinkers – Christians as well as Jews – still cast a blight upon the world. This was brought home most forcibly to Moses by a letter he received from Gotthold Lessing.

Lessing was still full of enthusiasm for Reimarus' *Defence of the Rational Worshippers of God,* and he told Moses that he was having it published under the title of *Fragments by an Anonymous Writer*. He didn't mention Moses' violent objections to the work, but merely told his friend that he was arranging for it to appear in instalments.

'He's including all the parts which will most shock the Church,' said Moses, aghast, as he began reading the *Fragments* which Lessing had enclosed with his letter. He and Fromet were spending a quiet afternoon at home, though 'quiet' was hardly the word for it while the five children were there!

Fromet was playing with their one-year-old son, Abraham, and she looked up enquiringly as her husband spoke. Dorothea and Recha, who were playing a card game with Henriette, and seven-year-old Joseph, stopped concentrating on the game and began to listen to their parents. The two older girls were highly intelligent, and, unlike their father, thoroughly enjoyed arguments.

'But that doesn't make any difference to us.' Dorothea was surprised at her father's obvious distress.

'Why should we mind, anyway?' demanded Recha, taking her cue from Dorothea's casual attitude.

Moses stared at his daughters and said sternly, 'Because this publication will shock and embitter Christians everywhere. It will shake their faith in their Church and its teachings, and will encourage young people to dismiss religion as old-fashioned and out-of-tune with modern eighteenth-century ideas. If

128

that happens, it will be a terrible thing. A religious outlook and faith in the God of one's ancestors is as *essential* to the human race as food and clothes.'

Dorothea and Recha shrugged their shoulders and turned their attention once more to the cards. They did not see why their father was so worried about a religion which was not his own; they did not understand he was simply afraid for the future.

Moses' worst fears proved justified. As soon as the *Fragments* reached the public, there was a tremendous outcry. The ideas expressed seemed so logical that young men in particular were profoundly influenced by them. But devout Christians were horrified by the publication; and because the author was not named the dispute grew violent and unpleasant. Many attacked Lessing; others suggested that the work had been written by Moses Mendelssohn himself, or that the Jews had arranged for it to be published!

Public opinion was so incensed that before long Lessing was forbidden to issue further instalments of the *Fragments*. He was made to leave his job as librarian, and soon was desperately in need of money. Then he had a brilliant idea: he would raise money by writing a play – a play that would annoy his critics even more than before!

Towards the end of 1778, Lessing finished what proved to be his greatest work, *Nathan the Wise*. The main character of the play, Nathan, who was a wise

129

B

and noble Jew, was modelled on Moses Mendelssohn himself. Lessing had always looked on Moses as the ideal Jew, and he wanted to embody all his friend's fine characteristics and virtues in the Jewish hero of his play.

As soon as he had finished it, Lessing sent the play to Moses and asked him for his opinion. Moses was delighted to receive it, and although he didn't get a chance to start reading it until late at night, he couldn't put it down until he had finished every word of it.

It was an exciting story, set in Jerusalem. After the Crusaders had killed his wife and children in a dreadful massacre, Nathan adopted a young orphaned Christian girl, named Recha. He brought her up with love and tenderness, and taught her to revere God.

But then the Sultan got to hear about Recha, and he angrily summoned Nathan to his palace to punish him for withholding the Christian religion from the child. But first he demanded an explanation from Nathan, and he asked him whether Judaism, Christianity or Islam was the true religion.

Nathan replied by telling the Sultan a story about a father who possessed a magic ring. Whoever owned and believed in the magic powers of the ring was dearly loved by God and by his fellow-men. The trouble was that the father did not know to which of his three sons he should give the ring when he died. In the end he decided to have two other rings made

130

exactly like the magic one, so no one could tell the difference between them.

After their father's death, the sons appealed to a judge to tell them which of the three rings was the true one. The judge said they should each believe his own to be the real ring, and to try and prove it by leading a noble and virtuous life which would make him beloved by God and man.

The Sultan was quick to see the point of Nathan's story. Of course it was obvious – every man should believe his *own* religion to be the true one, and to act in a way that would make him beloved by God and man.

When Moses came to the end of the play, he leaned back in his chair and smiled happily. Through the mouth of Lessing's hero, Nathan, the Christian world was about to have a telling lesson on religious tolerance.

CHAPTER TWELVE

Important Works

ONE day, in the spring of 1780, Moses received a disturbing message from his brother Saul, who still lived in Dessau. Their parents, who were now both in their seventies, had been in poor health for some time, and just lately they had been growing weaker. 'Nothing would give them greater happiness than to see you again,' wrote Saul in large, carefully outlined Hebrew characters. 'They talk about you all the time, for they are so proud of you. Do try and come back to Dessau soon.'

Moses at once sent word that he would be leaving Berlin within the next day or two, for he was as anxious to see his parents as they were to see him. His parents had always been so active; he hated to think of them burdened by age and illness.

Although he at once set about making plans for his journey, he was sorry to think he would have to leave his work. He was now involved in a mammoth task – that of translating the Five Books of Moses (the Pentateuch) from Hebrew into German. He had already translated the Psalms into German for the benefit of his own children, and he had decided to do the Pentateuch too after some persuasion from Solomon Dubno. Dubno, a tutor who had been with the Mendelssohns for some time, taught Hebrew grammar to Joseph and the girls. He knew how much they had gained from their father's translation of the Psalms, and he was positive that other children would also benefit if they could read the Pentateuch as well as the Psalms in German.

Moses and Fromet had always spoken German to each other and to their children, for they wanted them to be fluent in their native tongue. This meant that they had to learn Hebrew as a foreign language – a strange state of affairs for Jewish children of that time. Although Moses wanted them to be proud of their German nationality, he did not want them to be any the less proud of their religious faith.

The day before Moses left Berlin on the journey to Dessau he spent a couple of hours with Solomon Dubno discussing problems that might arise in his absence. The Book of Genesis had been finished a little while ago and they were now planning the next stage of the work. Dubno was writing a Hebrew commentary to Moses' translation of the Pentateuch which was intended to clarify any point that might puzzle the reader. After they had been talking for a while, Moses leaned back in his chair and stared intently at Dubno. 'What's wrong with you?' he asked, trying hard to keep the irritation from his voice. 'You were so keen to help me at first, but now you seem to have lost interest in the work.'

Dubno blushed slightly and looked uncomfortable. Then he said hesitatingly, 'Several very religious colleagues of mine have told me that our translation will harm Judaism. They say that Jewish children should only read Hebrew books. If they are taught to read German they may become interested in other books which are not about religion!'

Moses snorted indignantly. 'What rubbish your friends talk! Judaism won't suffer if our children are taught German. They'll be just as interested in their religion, and, if they do read about other subjects, then they'll simply be better educated. Surely you're not worrying over what your friends say? After all, it was partly your idea that I should translate the Five Books of Moses.'

'Oh, I'm still just as interested,' replied Dubno quickly. He did not want to annoy his employer, and, anyway, when he was talking to Moses he found himself easily convinced of the importance of their task.

Moses thought about his talk with Dubno quite a lot on the journey to Dessau. He knew the translation might meet with opposition, but this was not a reason for discontinuing it.

The only way a book could be published at that time was for the author, or other interested parties, to persuade people to subscribe for it – that is, to order and pay for copies before the book was printed. When Moses had decided to embark upon this task he had prepared a specimen of the work, which had appeared under his own name and at his own expense. Reaction to it had been swift and strong. Many rabbis, including the famous Rabbi Elijah of Wilna, had announced their approval, declaring that German Jews should know the language of the country in which they lived. They believed that such a translation would do much to stamp out this ignorance. For that very same reason, other rabbis considered the work would be harmful – and among those who held that view was Raphael Cohen of Altona (which then lay in the King of Denmark's realm). They were afraid that if Jews became familiar with the German language they would in time want to have synagogue services held in German instead of Hebrew. These rabbis denounced the book and forbade their congregants to read it.

However, both the King and the Crown Prince of Denmark agreed to subscribe for the translation – greatly to the annoyance of Rabbi Raphael Cohen! And despite the opposition from various other quarters subscriptions had come in from all parts of Germany, as well as from Jews in England, France, Holland and Poland.

Just then, the coach began to clatter across the wooden bridge spanning the River Mulde. Moses sat up eagerly, and thrust his problems aside. Here he was, back in Dessau, the town of his childhood. All he could think about were his parents, and his brothers and their wives and families, and the joy and the excitement they would share during his few days' visit.

Moses' parents had indeed grown frail, but when they saw their son they seemed to take on a new lease of life. During the past thirty-seven years they had seen Moses very seldom, but they had thought and talked about him a great deal. They were proud to think he had made a name for himself in an intellectual world which was entirely strange to them. Now that he was with them again they were anxious to hear all that he had done and was planning to do; but of course, at first, they talked only of themselves and of Fromet and the family.

The visit passed all too quickly. Moses hated leaving his parents, but both he and they knew that his place was in Berlin. Herr Mendel had been particularly interested in the translation of the Pentateuch and Moses promised to send him a printed copy as soon as possible.

With fond cries of 'Good luck, good-bye and God bless you!' ringing in his ears, Moses left his parents' home a few days later, in time to catch the coach which travelled weekly to Berlin. He had enjoyed every moment of his stay in Dessau, and though he was sorry to leave his parents he was eager to be home with Fromet and the children once more. And, of course, to be back among his beloved books and to be working once more on the Pentateuch.

During the journey he let his thoughts stray happily to the welcome he would receive when he arrived home. Fromet always made a great fuss of him after he'd been away for any length of time, and he was sure that to-day would be no exception.

But a shock was in store for him. When he reached home he found the place in an uproar. Fromet was in tears, Dorothea, Recha, Henriette and Joseph were rushing madly around – and Solomon Dubno was practically hysterical! Bewildered, Moses stared at them all, and then he sank wearily into a chair in the hall. 'What on earth . . . ?' he began, but was interrupted when everyone tried to answer him at once.

'Brigands! Bandits! Burglars!' shrieked Joseph excitedly.

'Thieves . . . they've broken into the house . . .' sobbed Fromet.

White-faced and trembling, Dubno muttered, 'It's the work of the devil! It's judgment upon us . . . upon me . . . upon you. . . .'

Moses was angry. 'Have you gone mad?' he demanded of Dubno. 'If we've had burglars, we've had *burglars*, not the devil! Anyway, what's been stolen?'

Dubno stared fearfully at Moses, but said nothing.

'Your study . . .' said Fromet chokingly. 'They've broken into your study . . . the parchments with your work on the Pentateuch. . . .'

'WHAT!' Moses leapt up from his chair, and rushed towards his study. The door was open, and the floor was littered with sheets of parchment. His carefully-written notes, which he had left in neat piles, had disappeared from the desk.

Frantically he fumbled among his belongings to see what else had gone. He pushed aside the chairs, and looked in the bookcases. He gathered up the sheets which were on the floor, and hastily examined them. Fromet stood by, watching anxiously.

Moses wrinkled his brows. 'I don't understand this at all. Everything is here, except for two very important sheets of notes. . . .'

'Father! Father!' Joseph's high-pitched voice rang out from the upstairs landing. Moses and Fromet then heard him jumping down the stairs. A second later he burst into the room. 'Look! Look what I've got!' He held out two sheets of parchment.

'My notes! The missing notes! Thank goodness you've found them!'

'Where were they?' croaked out Dubno, who had been standing silently in the background.

Joseph went off into peals of laughter. 'In Abraham's cradle! I heard him crying just now, went in to see him, and found him clutching them. Do you remember, Mother, you sent Dorothea to look for him this afternoon? He must have got into Father's study. He could easily have reached the desk. . . .'

Joseph was now roaring with laughter. Then, so great was everyone's relief that they all joined in – even the solemn Solomon Dubno!

'That's the end of that!' said Moses thankfully to Fromet. But he was wrong.

Two days later Dubno told him that he had decided to return to his home in Poland. He was sorry not to be able to continue the commentary, but he was sure Moses could easily find another scholar to help him with the remaining books.

The children teased him unmercifully, for they were convinced that Dubno still thought that the devil, and not their young brother, was responsible for the chaotic state of the study. But Moses understood that Dubno was under very great pressure from his religious colleagues in Berlin. For weeks they had tried to convince him that his work on the Pentateuch was a grave disservice to Judaism, and now it appeared that they had succeeded. However, Moses refused to allow himself to be disheartened, and at once began to think of other scholars who might assist him.

Three years later, in 1783, the translation of the entire Pentateuch, and also of the Psalms, appeared before the public. At once there was a tremendous outcry.

Christian thinkers recognised its merit, and many of them praised it. The reception it received from Jewish theologians was just as varied as Moses had expected: some violently opposed it, while others greatly approved. But the people who welcomed it most were young Talmudic students, who seized upon the translation and studied it avidly – even when they were strictly forbidden to do so by their tutors. Gradually, through the Hebrew commentary,

139

these students became familiar with the German language, and found as a result that many new fields of study were opened up to them.

There was no doubt that Moses' translation of the Pentateuch was striking a deadly blow at the narrow-minded mentality which had prevailed for centuries past. It was as though a dam had just been broken, and a tremendous and uncontrollable desire for knowledge was engulfing the Jewish people. Once this book was published, there was no looking back. The ghetto walls which had constricted the minds of men began to crumble: progress and enlightenment were now assured.

Moses was responsible for another great advance in the world of education even before the Pentateuch had been completed. In 1781 he persuaded some of his wealthy friends to found a Jewish school in Berlin. He found it hard to convince everyone that, besides the Bible and Talmud, the children should be taught technical subjects as well as German and French. But finally he did so, and to his great delight, the experiment proved an outstanding success. This was the first organised Jewish school to be started in Germany, and as the years went by others sprang up modelled upon it.

Although Moses had put so much time and effort during the last five years into his work on the Pentateuch, he still managed to think of other things. He was always horrified to hear of the sufferings of Jews in other parts of Europe, and, whenever he could, he did his best to help. One day he received a deputation from the Jewish community in the German-speaking province of Alsace, which then belonged to France. He was told about the oppression which twenty thousand of his co-religionists had endured for so long. In desperation these people had decided to appeal to their King, Louis XVI, and they wanted Moses to draw up a petition describing their sufferings. They thought that even the King would not disregard a plea from so renowned a philosopher as Moses Mendelssohn.

Moses was very sorry for them, and promised to see what he could do. He contacted a Christian friend, William Dohm, who was a historian and had recently been appointed by King Frederick the Great to the post of Keeper of the Archives. Moses persuaded Dohm to write a pamphlet summarising the past history of the Jews in Europe, and telling of the false accusations and persecutions which they had had to endure.

Dohm was very enthusiastic about it all. He was glad to help because he had always thought that the usual attitude of scorn towards the Jews was most unreasonable. As he said in his pamphlet, persecution of the Jews could not be justified on the grounds that they followed a religion of harmful doctrines, for 'the chief book of the Jews, the Law of Moses, is regarded with reverence also by Christians'.

Dohm's pamphlet was called *Upon the Civil Amelioration of the Condition of the Jews,* and was

141

published in August 1781. It succeeded in arousing some interest in Jewish problems from Christian scholars, clergymen, politicians and even princes, but Moses felt he could not yet allow the matter to rest. So he persuaded a friend to translate into German *The Defence of the Jews* (*Vindiciae Judaeorum*) by Menasseh ben Israel, the Dutch rabbi who in 1655 had gone to London to beg Oliver Cromwell to re-admit the Jews into England, and Moses himself wrote a preface pleading for justice and toleration.

But more was to come from Moses' pen. As well as translating the Pentateuch, Moses had for some time been engrossed on a new work. This was called *Jerusalem or Upon Ecclesiastical Power and Judaism,* and was published in the spring of 1783. It brought even more fame to Moses, and, what was to him of far greater importance, had a profound effect on religious thinking. In *Jerusalem* Moses pleaded for religious toleration, and defined the different functions of the Church and State in Germany. He spoke, too, of the dual responsibility of a Jew—his duty to his religion and to his native land. And his advice to the Jews of the eighteenth century is as true to-day as it was then : 'Adapt yourselves to the manners and the constitution of the country in which you live; but hold fast also to the religion of your fathers! Carry both burdens as well as you can. . . .

'I do not see how those who are born in the house of Jacob can in any way conscientiously throw off the law.'

CHAPTER THIRTEEN

His Last Task

MOSES leaned back in his chair and smiled at his daughter. 'Everything's arranged, Dorothea. Simon Veit is a nice young man, and banking is a steady profession. He wants to marry you in April, and I have given my consent.'

'But I haven't given mine!' retorted Dorothea, her eyes flashing angrily. 'I don't want to marry Simon. He may be nice, but he's an awful bore! Why can't I choose my own husband?'

Moses was astonished at this outburst. Simon would make Dorothea an excellent husband. How could she be so ungrateful! She was now nineteen years of age. Of course she must marry! Patiently he explained this to her, but, when she seemed no more convinced than before, he said sternly, 'I am your father, and I know best. You will marry Simon in April, and I wish to hear no more arguments from you!'

Dorothea rushed from the room, and slammed the

door as loudly as possible. Recha, who was standing on the landing, stared anxiously at her sister as she marched up the stairs. 'Wasn't it any use?'

Dorothea shook her head. 'None at all. I don't understand Father. He's usually so tolerant and understanding, but now he's adamant. Why should I marry a man whom I hardly know? Anyway if I did know him better, I'm quite sure I should want to marry him even less!'

Recha, who, at seventeen, was still conventional, felt rather shocked at Dorothea's attitude. Of course a husband must be chosen by one's parents . . . none of their friends were allowed to make up their own minds . . . it just wasn't done!

Dorothea and Recha had no chance to discuss this further because they had to get ready for their parents' soirée, which was about to start. The Mendelssohns frequently held such parties in their home, and many brilliant men and beautiful women would be among their guests. These soirées were very formal affairs, and Dorothea and Recha thoroughly enjoyed wearing their finest gowns, and helping their parents entertain the visitors. Dorothea, especially, loved talking to clever, witty people and had always been certain that she would marry the most intelligent man of them all. But now her husband was to be Simon – a pretty poor substitute for an intellectual professor! Gloomily she asked, 'Is anyone interesting coming to the soirée?'

Recha shook her head. 'No, I don't think so, except

for a young and very poor Polish student called Solomon Maimon. He's written to Father once or twice, and he's coming here this evening.'

Dorothea took a final look at herself in the mirror. She smoothed down the folds in her long satin dress, patted the curls in her elaborate coiffure, and added a little more powder and rouge to her soft, creamy complexion. 'Come on, we'd better hurry. I'm sure I can hear some guests arriving.'

Gracefully the two young women descended the stairs and entered the salon. Immediately they were drawn into separate groups, and began to enjoy themselves.

Their father, meanwhile, was standing in the hall and was about to come into the salon when he saw the front door being pushed open. An untidy-looking young man, wearing crumpled clothes and dirty shoes, looked uncertainly around, then gaped and stepped back. Moses hurried forward and pulled the door open again. 'Herr Maimon,' he cried to the young man, who was now hurrying away down the drive.

Solomon Maimon paused, turned round, and slowly walked back.

'Come in, come in,' said Moses hospitably. 'I've been looking forward to meeting you and to hearing more about the views which you outlined in your letters to me. Surely you're not going to rush away?'

Nervously Maimon entered the house. He felt very

self-conscious, and his awkwardness increased as he glanced into the drawing-room and saw the beautifully dressed women and the bewigged and frock-coated men standing around in groups, talking and laughing.

'Perhaps I shouldn't have come,' muttered Maimon. 'I haven't any better clothes to wear. . . .'

Moses briskly interrupted. 'Neither had I when I first came to Berlin. Let's sit over there by the window, and we can talk together quietly.'

A few of the guests glanced curiously at Moses as he sat listening intently to the young man beside him. But they were used to seeing enthusiastic, though impoverished students at the Mendelssohns', and this latest visitor did not arouse much interest. After all, how were they to know that in the years to come Solomon Maimon would make his name in the world of philosophy?

From their conversation Moses could see that Maimon had a real understanding of metaphysical problems, though he had been hampered in his work by a scarcity of books. He offered to make arrangements for Maimon's board and lodgings, and to get permission for him to use various libraries. Maimon thanked him warmly, and then said he thought he ought to be going. He felt ill at ease in these comfortable surroundings and was more than ever conscious of his muddy boots and shabby clothes.

Moses suggested a time for him to call again, and then saw his guest to the door. He smiled kindly at

Maimon, who made his departure in an awkward and ungainly manner.

Still smiling, Moses turned back into the house and walked towards the drawing-room. He stood in the doorway unnoticed for a few moments, quite content with his own thoughts. Maimon had told him how he had been refused entrance into Berlin on the first occasion he had come to the Rosenthal Gate. Vivid memories came flooding back to Moses . . . especially of the time when he himself stood trembling at the gate, confronted by that fearful watchman!

How times had changed, and how great had been his fortune! His early years in Berlin had been full of hardships, yet he had managed to earn enough for himself, and later for his wife and family, and still find time to study. He and Fromet had known great happiness in the little house on the outskirts of Berlin where they had first set up home. Now they possessed a much finer abode, with large suites of rooms downstairs and plenty of accommodation in the floors above for their children.

Moses glanced round the drawing-room, and his eyes rested on Dorothea who was talking animatedly to her closest friend, Henriette Herz. Then he stopped reminiscing, and turned his mind to the question of her marriage. He was sorry to see Dorothea almost ignoring Simon, who stood contentedly by her side, gazing at her as though he were bewitched by her beauty.

If Dorothea had hoped that Simon himself would

change his mind, she was to be disappointed. Her fate was settled, and in April of the following year – 1783 – she was betrothed to Simon. It was a gay, happy occasion for all the family, and in the bustle and excitement of it all even Dorothea seemed content.

About this time Moses began to find the strain of everyday life almost too much for him. Although two years had now passed since he had heard the news of the death of his closest friend, Lessing, he had never really recovered from the blow. As the months went by, he began to think more and more about him. Then he made up his mind to write a sketch of Lessing as a memorial to the man who had meant so much to him.

Many stories and anecdotes about Lessing were told by all the intellectuals, but there was one which horrified Moses. It was said that Lessing had secretly been an admirer of Spinoza, the seventeenth-century philosopher, who was excommunicated by the Jewish community in Amsterdam for not observing religious laws. One of the people who was spreading this tale was the brilliant philosopher, F. H. Jacobi. Moses wrote to him, but received a reply that was so complicated that he found great difficulty in understanding it. His physical weakness made strenuous mental effort almost an impossibility.

One evening, long after the children were in bed, Fromet came into her husband's study. It was very late, she was tired, and knew Moses must be worn out. Fromet felt a queer stab at her heart when she saw Moses sitting at his desk, one hand wearily supporting his head. The flickering oil lamp, which cast its shadows across his face, gave Moses the appearance of an old and dying man.

Fromet tried to keep the anxiety out of her voice. 'Darling, it's so late. Please come to bed.'

Moses looked up and smiled rather sadly at his wife. His work was proving such an effort. He was anxious to complete it, yet at the same time he felt concerned that he was not devoting enough time to Fromet and the children. 'I wanted to get started on an essay to-night, but my brain seems to have stopped working.'

'It's because you're tired,' said Fromet soothingly. 'If only you will get some rest to-night, you are sure to feel better to-morrow. Must you keep on?'

Moses rubbed his eyes. He had strained them so much that he could hardly see clearly. 'I wanted to publish a reply to Jacobi's accusations against Lessing. I must defend Lessing. I cannot believe that he admired Spinoza's philosophy, that he doubted the truth of a personal God, of providence, and of immortality. Surely he would have told me – his closest friend?' Moses sat with his head bowed, but with an uncomfortable thought flashing through his mind. Perhaps Lessing had deceived him.

No, it was not possible. Moses pulled himself together and sat bolt upright. He would start at once on

149

his pamphlet, which he would call *To the Friends of Lessing*.

'Fromet, I must work for a little longer,' said Moses firmly, though his brain was still confused with different thoughts. He picked up his quill pen, and with his hand trembling from sheer tiredness he began to put his ideas on paper.

Fromet anxiously watched him for a few moments. She could see further argument would be useless. Moses seemed determined to work – even if he dropped. Sadly she left him alone, and went up to bed.

In the morning Moses insisted on getting up early and returning to his study. Only with difficulty did Fromet persuade him to leave his desk and join his family for meals. But as soon as they had finished eating, he went back to his study and continued working feverishly.

The children were as worried as their mother. Joseph went round to see Dorothea—who lived fairly close to her parents' home – to ask whether she would try to make their father rest. 'He's straining himself terribly,' said Joseph. 'He'll break down completely if he carries on like this. Mother's done her best to stop him, but he won't listen.'

'I don't think I've got any influence over him,' replied Dorothea somewhat bitterly. After all, her father hadn't listened to her when she had told him she didn't want to marry Simon! Oh, Simon was kind enough, she knew that, but he wasn't a man who could make her really happy. 'Why is he working so hard, anyway?'

Joseph, who was now a slim, good-looking boy of sixteen, leaned forward in his chair and frowned deeply. 'Jacobi has published something about Lessing which is supposed to prove that he was an admirer of Spinoza. He used some of Father's private letters – without his knowledge or permission – to try to prove his point. In his pamphlet, Father explains that if Lessing had admired Spinoza, he would only have agreed with the philosophy in its most refined form, which is not in any way anti-Jewish. Father also gives his own objections to Spinoza's philosophy.'

Dorothea looked thoughtful. 'The pamphlet sounds a good idea to me. I've heard of the rumours which Jacobi has been spreading about Lessing, and I think Father's quite right to defend the man who was his life-long friend.'

Joseph sighed, not only from worry about his father, but also out of sadness for the way in which Dorothea seemed to have changed. She had always been interested in literature and learning, but now her views on the importance of intellectual achievement had grown out of all proportion. With unusual feeling in his voice, he said, 'Dorothea, please try and persuade him to ease up a little. You'll understand when you see how ill he looks.'

Evidently Joseph had misjudged his sister, for the moment he had finished speaking she laid a hand on one of his, and said reassuringly, 'Of course I'll come and see what I can do, though I understand why Father feels he must reply to Jacobi.'

'Mother had hoped that *Morning Hours* would be the last of Father's works to be published. She is afraid he is wearing himself out.'

Morning Hours, to which Joseph referred, was a collection of discourses. Moses used to give talks every morning to his children and some of their friends, and he would explain his philosophy and religious beliefs. He then decided to have the discourses published, and these appeared in 1784.

After Joseph had left, Dorothea began to feel concerned about her father. She finished her daily tasks, and as soon as the household was in order, she called for her carriage and was driven to her parents' home.

Fromet welcomed her daughter with open arms, but it was evident that she was distraught. But of one thing she was certain, and that was that Moses must not be disturbed. 'I promised your father that he would not be interrupted to-day. I tried to make him rest yesterday, but he says it worries him when we fuss. There's nothing we can do, but wait for him to finish. Lessing was such a good friend to your father, and meant so much to him, and I know he won't stop working until he has cleared Lessing's name.'

Dorothea shivered and held her hands in front of the fire. They were sitting in the drawing-room, where the maid had just brought in some tea. The curtains had been drawn, and there was a feeling of warmth and comfort in the room, though outside, on this December day in 1785, there was snow and ice and a keen, biting wind.

'Is this pamphlet going to take much longer,' asked Dorothea, as she leaned back against the cushions and thankfully sipped the hot tea.

For a moment, a look of relief appeared on her mother's lined face. 'I don't think so. He said yesterday that he only needed another few hours to complete it.'

At that moment, they heard a door open. Fromet started, then sighed with relief. 'Oh, thank goodness,' she breathed. 'He must have finished. He would never have come in to join us if he still had more to do,' Fromet explained as they heard Moses walking slowly across the hall.

When Moses entered the room, an expression of horror came over Dorothea's face. Her father looked desperately white and wizened, and he was walking with an effort. But he was smiling, and seemed content. 'At last I've finished my reply to Jacobi.'

'I'm so pleased,' Fromet said happily. 'Come and sit down and I'll pour you out some tea.'

'In a minute,' said Moses, his mind not entirely with her. 'I must first take the manuscript round to the publishers.'

'Father, you can't go out in this weather,' protested Dorothea. 'It's freezing and. . . .'

Moses brushed her protests aside. He was glad he

had finished the work, and he had told Voss, his publisher, that he would have it in his hands by December 31st. He wanted to give it to him personally, and then he would be able to rest. 'I'll wrap up warmly, and will be back soon.'

Dorothea turned to her mother. 'He mustn't go out into the snow . . . if only I hadn't sent my carriage away. Make him wait until to-morrow.'

But Moses was determined. He put on a thick top-coat, and made his way down the drive. The biting wind made him gasp, but he did not falter. He clutched the precious pages of his manuscript more tightly and staggered down the icy street.

Anxiously his family waited at home for him to return.

CHAPTER FOURTEEN

Time of Sorrow

A N hour later, Moses was back, Dorothea opened the drawing-room door, and her father almost fell into the room. Fromet rushed forward, and together they helped him to reach the chair by the fire.

Moses was breathing in quick gasps, his face was deathly white, and he put his hand to his heart as though he were in severe pain. Fromet knelt by his side, and whispered, 'Moses, what has happened to you?'

Her husband managed a wan smile. 'Nothing . . . don't worry . . . I'll be better in a moment. It was colder than I thought. I felt a sharp pain when I left the house – I thought it would go once I started walking – but now it seems worse than before.' He was speaking with an effort, but at last a little colour was coming back into his face.

'Perhaps you've caught a cold,' suggested Fromet, trying to make light of her fear. Never, she thought,

155

had she seen Moses look so ill! 'Let me help you up the stairs, then you can rest in bed.'

Moses walked slowly from the room, leaning thankfully on Fromet's arm. With difficulty he climbed the stairs to his room. Within a few minutes he was lying between the covers of the draped four-poster bed, while the servant had gone scuttling down the stairs to fetch the copper bed-warming pans. Fromet brought a chair to the bedside, and sat with her husband for the short time it took him to fall asleep.

Dorothea had been waiting downstairs in the drawing-room. Despite her resentment at the way her father had arranged her marriage, her affection for him had in no way been dimmed. She looked up anxiously as her mother came into the room, and sighed with relief when Fromet said, 'He's sleeping peacefully now, and I'm sure he'll be all right in a day or two. He's been working far too hard, but he has promised me that he will rest. If he doesn't seem better soon, I'll send for the doctor.'

Just then there was a knock at the front door. 'That must be Simon – I told him I would be visiting you this afternoon,' said Dorothea, going over to the window and pulling the curtains aside. 'Yes, I can see his carriage. I hope Father's quite recovered to-morrow, but anyway I'll come and see you.'

Simon's arrival was then announced by the maid, and Dorothea walked over to greet him. She told him briefly about her father's near-collapse. He was very concerned and asked Fromet to send for him at any time if he could be of help. She assured him that she would, though felt certain there would be no need. Soon afterwards Dorothea and Simon left.

Three days later Joseph called on his sister after he had finished his work at the office. He told them that Moses still didn't seem well, but insisted on getting up each day and coming downstairs to sit on the sofa by the fire. 'Luckily he's given up any idea of working, and he seems quite content just to stay and watch Mother sewing and to talk to us all.'

'We'll come round to-morrow evening,' promised Dorothea.

But she and Simon came before that. The following morning, before they had had breakfast, an urgent knocking at the door brought Simon hurriedly downstairs to find young Abraham, distraught and out-of-breath, standing outside. 'Come quickly,' he cried, before Simon had a chance to speak. 'Father's very ill, and Joseph's gone to fetch the doctor.'

Hurriedly the Veits finished dressing, while the servant ran to the stables. Soon the carriage was at the door, and Dorothea, Simon and Abraham clambered inside. They urged the coachman to hurry, and sat impatiently as the coach clattered over the cobbled streets.

When they arrived, the doctor was already there. They waited in the study to hear his verdict, but he came into the room and sadly shook his head. Moses' health had never been good, and the many years of

unceasing strain to which his body had been sub-
jected had at last taken their toll. The doctor warned
them that the end was near.

A few hours later on the same day – 3rd January,
1786 – with his loving family surrounding him, the
life of Moses Mendelssohn drew peacefully to a close.

Fromet and her children were overwhelmed with
grief. They could hardly believe that Moses was with
them no more. The days that followed were bitter,
but gradually they became adjusted to his death, and
could remember him in love and not in sadness.

They spent much of their time reading and re-
reading Moses' works. And when they came across a
paragraph which he had written nineteen years before, they felt strangely comforted. For in 1767,
Moses had declared: 'As for myself, I am contented
with the conviction that God's eyes are ever upon me,
that His Providence and justice will follow me into
the future life as it has protected me in this, and that
my true happiness consists in the development of the
powers of my soul. It is such felicity that awaits me
in the life to come. More I do not desire to know.'

CHAPTER FIFTEEN

Looking Back

MOSES' widow and children were not alone
in their sorrow: countless numbers of people
in Germany and in many other lands mourned the
passing of a great and noble man. His early struggles
and his later achievements stirred the imagina-
tion of all who admired courage, and who could
recognise outstanding qualities of character and
intellect.

His life stands out as a milestone in our history.
For centuries past, the Jews in Germany had been
persecuted, scorned and despised – and few had been
able to rise above their unhappy circumstances. It
was largely due to Moses Mendelssohn that they
were at last able to escape from the mental stagna-
tion of the ghetto. For his translation of the Pentateuch helped them to learn German, and once they
had overcome this hurdle, they could then broaden
their outlook and improve their education. This in
its turn led to the Jews being gradually assimilated

into German culture and accepted as equals by their Gentile neighbours.

Moses Mendelssohn devoted his life to the cause of learning, and at all times strove to bring progress and enlightenment to European Jewry. The battles that he fought, and the victories that he won, make him a true hero of our people.